REGENCY EDITION

spdr

srhN

dcgre

REGENCY EDITION

spdri

srthN

*dcyre**

JOE M. PULLIS, Ed.D.
Professor, Department of Office Administration
and Business Communication
College of Administration and Business
Louisiana Tech University

Glencoe Publishing Company
Mission Hills, California

*SPEEDWRITING
SHORTHAND
DICTIONARY
(abridged)

Cheryl D. Pullis, M. Ed.
System Consultant

Calligraphy: Juana Silcox
Cover and interior design: Harkavy Publishing Services/Levavi & Levavi
System editor: Karl C. Illg, Jr.
Typesetter: Compolith Graphics
Printer: R. R. Donnelley

Send all inquiries to:
Glencoe Publishing Company
15319 Chatsworth Street
Mission Hills, California 91345

Printed in the United States of America

Library of Congress Cataloging in Publication Data

Pullis, Joe M.

  Spdri srthN dcjre = Speedwriting shorthand dictionary (abridged)
  1. Shorthand—Speedwriting—Dictionaries.   I. Title.   II. Title: Speedwriting shorthand
dictionary (abridged)
Z56.2.S6A3 1984   653'.2'0321   83-22517

ISBN 0-02-679660-0
          6 7   90 89 88

CONTENTS

WORD DIVISION RULES

The *Speedwriting Shorthand Abridged Dictionary*, *Regency Edition*, contains shorthand outlines for over 6,000 of the most frequently used words in business communications, and all places where these words can correctly be divided in typewriting transcription applications are shown. The rules utilized for these word divisions are as follows.

1. Divide words only between syllables: dis·play, con·scious
   Thus, one-syllable words cannot be divided: strength, through

2. Do not divide a word of five or fewer letters: ideas, refer

3. Do not divide a proper noun, a contraction, an abbreviation, or a figure:
   America, shouldn't, A.S.P.C.A., $10,234.75

4. Do not divide a one- or two-letter syllable at the end of a word: ready, lively.

5. Retain as much of a word as possible on the first line; otherwise, retain at least two letters of a word on the first line.

6. Whenever possible, divide a word after its prefix or before its suffix:
   dis·or·gan·ize, set·tle·ment

   Preferred: dis·organize, settle·ment

7. Whenever possible, divide a compound word between the elements of the compound: busi·ness·woman, over·produc·tion

   Preferred: business·woman, over·production

8. Divide hyphenated words at the hyphen only: self-assured, sister-in-law

9. Divide words between double consonants when a suffix is added unless the root word itself ends in double letters, in which case division is made after the double letters: small·est, fill·ing, miss·ing, big·gest, con·trol·ling, mis·sion

10. Divide a word between two consecutive single-vowel syllables:
    con·tinu·ation, situ·ation

11. In general, retain an internal single-vowel with the first part of a word: sepa·rate, elimi·nate

    But, divide before a single-vowel if that syllable is part of the word ending forms of *able* or *ible, icle* or *ical, ity* or *ety:* pay·able, med·ical, abil·ity

    Also, divide before a single-vowel syllable if that syllable is part of a root word which contains a prefix: dis·agree, dis·avow

12. Retain the single vowel *i* with *za* in nouns ending in ization: or·gan·iza·tion, au·thor·iza·tion

    The reference source used for syllabication of words was *The American Heritage Dictionary of the English Language, New College Edition* (Houghton Mifflin Company, Boston).

A

Word	Outline	Word	Outline
a	_____	academy	acdre
a.m.	a⌒	ac·cel·era·tor	lrar
aban·doned	abNn-	ac·cept	ac
abey·ance	abaN	ac·cept·able	acB
abil·ities	Bls	ac·cep·tance	acN
abil·ity	Bl	ac·cepted	ac-
able	B	ac·cept·ing	ac̲
ably	Bl	ac·cepts	acs
ab·nor·mal	abnrl	ac·cess	s
aboard	abrd	ac·ces·so·ries	sres
about	ab	ac·ci·dent	dN
above	abv	ac·ci·den·tal	dNl
abroad	abrd	ac·ci·dents	dNs
ab·sence	absN	ac·com·mo·date	akda
ab·sences	absNs	ac·com·mo·dat·ing	akda̲
ab·so·lute	abslu	ac·com·mo·da·tions	akdjs
ab·so·lutely	abslul	ac·com·pa·nied	aco-
ab·sorb	absrb	ac·com·pa·nies	acos
ab·stract	abSrc	ac·com·pa·ni·ment	acom
abun·dant	abNN	ac·com·pa·nist	acoS
aca·demic	acdrc	ac·com·pany	aco
		ac·com·pa·ny·ing	aco̲
		ac·com·plish	ak

Word	Outline	Word	Outline
ac·com·plished	*ak-*	ac·cu·rate	*acrl*
ac·com·plish·ing	*ak_*	ac·cu·rately	*acrll*
ac·com·plish·ment	*akm*	achieve	*aCv*
ac·com·plish·ments	*akms*	achieved	*aCv-*
ac·cord	*acrd*	achieve·ment	*aCvm*
ac·cord·ance	*acrdN*	achieve·ments	*aCvms*
ac·cord·ing	*acrd_*	achiev·ing	*aCv_*
ac·cord·ingly	*acrdl*	ac·knowl·edge	*acj*
ac·count	*ak*	ac·knowl·edged	*acj-*
ac·count·ant	*akN*	ac·knowl·edges	*acjs*
ac·count·ants	*akNs*	ac·knowl·edg·ing	*acj_*
ac·count·ing	*ak_*	ac·knowl·edg·ment	*acjm*
ac·counts	*aks*	ac·knowl·edg·ments	*acjms*
ac·credit	*acr*	ac·quaint	*aqN*
ac·credi·ta·tion	*acrj*	ac·quain·tance	*aqNN*
ac·cred·ited	*acr-*	ac·quainted	*aqN-*
ac·cred·it·ing	*acr_*	ac·quire	*aq*
ac·cred·its	*acrs*	ac·quired	*aq-*
ac·crued	*acru-*	ac·quir·ing	*aq_*
ac·cu·mu·late	*acula*	ac·qui·si·tion	*aqzj*
ac·cu·mu·lated	*acula-*	ac·qui·si·tions	*aqzjs*
ac·cu·mu·la·tion	*aculj*	acre	*acr*
ac·cu·racy	*acrse*	acre·age	*acrj*

Word	Shorthand	Word	Shorthand
acres	*acrs*	ad·di·tional	*adyl*
across	*acrs*	ad·di·tion·ally	*adyll*
acrylic	*acrlc*	ad·di·tions	*adys*
act	*ac*	ad·dress	*adrs Ars* (N. or V. / N.)
acted	*ac-*	ad·dressed	*adrs-*
act·ing	*ac_*	ad·dresser	*adrsr*
ac·tion	*acy*	ad·dress·ers	*adrsrs*
ac·tions	*acys*	ad·dresses	*adrss Arss* (N. or V. / N.)
ac·tive	*acv*	ad·dress·ing	*adrs_*
ac·tively	*acvl*	adds	*As*
ac·tiv·ities	*acv⁶*	ade·quate	*Aql*
ac·tiv·ity	*acv¹*	ade·quately	*Aqll*
acts	*acs*	ad·ja·cent	*ajsN*
ac·tual	*acCul*	ad·joins	*ayns*
ac·tu·ally	*acCull*	ad·just	*ajS*
ac·tu·arial	*acCurel*	ad·justed	*ajS-*
acute	*acu*	ad·juster	*ajSr*
ad	*A*	ad·just·ers	*ajSrs*
adapt·able	*adplB*	ad·just·ing	*ajS_*
add	*A*	ad·just·ment	*ajSm*
added	*A-*	ad·just·ments	*ajSms*
add·ing	*A_*	ad·min·is·ter	*AmSr*
ad·di·tion	*ady*	ad·min·is·tered	*AmSr-*

Word	Shorthand	Word	Shorthand
ad·min·is·ter·ing	*Amsr*	ad·vance·ment	*Avnm*
ad·min·is·trate	*Am*	ad·vances	*Avns*
ad·min·is·trates	*Ams*	ad·van·tage	*Avj*
ad·min·is·trat·ing	*Am*	ad·van·ta·geous	*Avjs*
ad·min·is·tra·tion	*Amj*	ad·van·tages	*Avjs*
ad·min·is·tra·tions	*Amjs*	ad·verse	*Avrs*
ad·min·is·tra·tive	*Amv*	ad·versely	*Avrsl*
ad·min·is·tra·tor	*Amr*	ad·ver·tise	*Av*
ad·min·is·tra·tors	*Amrs*	ad·ver·tised	*Av-*
ad·mis·sion	*Aj*	ad·ver·tise·ment	*Avm*
ad·mis·sions	*Ajs*	ad·ver·tise·ments	*Avms*
admit	*Adl*	ad·ver·tiser	*Avr*
ad·mit·ted	*Adl-*	ad·ver·tises	*Avs*
ado·les·cent	*AlsN*	ad·ver·tis·ing	*Av_*
ado·les·cents	*AlsNs*	ad·vice	*Avs*
adopt	*adpl*	ad·vis·abil·ity	*Avzβ^l*
adopted	*adpl-*	ad·vis·able	*Avzβ*
adop·tion	*adpj*	ad·vise	*Avz*
ads	*As*	ad·vised	*Avz-*
adult	*adll*	ad·vises	*Avzs*
adults	*adlls*	ad·vis·ing	*Avz_*
ad·vance	*Avn*	ad·vi·sory	*Avzre*
ad·vanced	*Avn-*	aero·space	*arsps*

af·fairs	*afrs*	again	*ag*
af·fect	*afc*	against	*ag*
af·fected	*afc-*	age	*aj*
af·fect·ing	*afc̲*	aged	*aj-*
af·fi·da·vit	*afdvt*	agen·cies	*ajnes*
af·fi·da·vits	*afdvts*	agency	*ajne*
af·fili·ate	*află aflē̆t* (V.) (N.)	agenda	*ajna*
af·fili·ated	*afla-*	agent	*ajn*
af·fili·ation	*afley*	agents	*ajns*
af·fixed	*afx-*	ages	*ajs*
af·ford	*afd*	ag·gre·gate	*agrgt agrga* (adj.) (v.)
af·forded	*afd-*	ago	*ag*
af·ford·ing	*afd̲*	agree	*agre*
af·fords	*afds*	agree·able	*agreß*
afore·said	*afsd*	agreed	*agre-*
afraid	*afrd*	agree·ment	*agrem*
after	*af*	agree·ments	*agrems*
af·ter·math	*aft*	agrees	*agres*
af·ter·noon	*afnn*	ag·ri·cul·tural	*agrl*
af·ter·noons	*afnns*	ag·ri·cul·tur·ally	*agrll*
af·ter·thought	*aftt*	ag·ri·cul·ture	*agr*
af·ter·ward	*afw*	a·head	*ahd*
af·ter·wards	*afws*	aid	*ad*

Word	Shorthand	Word	Shorthand
aids	*ads*	al·lo·cated	*Aca-*
aim	*a—*	al·lo·ca·tion	*Acy*
aimed	*a—-*	al·lot·ment	*Altm*
air	*ar*	al·lot·ted	*Alt-*
air·craft	*arcrft*	allow	*alo*
air·line	*arln*	al·low·able	*aloB*
air·lines	*arlns*	al·low·ance	*aloN*
air·port	*arpt*	al·low·ances	*aloNs*
air·ports	*arpts*	al·lowed	*alo-*
air·ways	*ar as*	al·low·ing	*alo̲*
alarm	*alr—*	al·lows	*alos*
album	*Ab—*	al·most	*A—S*
al·bums	*Ab—s*	alone	*aln*
al·co·hol	*Achl*	along	*alg*
al·co·holic	*Achlc*	along·side	*algsd*
alert	*alrt*	al·pha·bet	*Afbt*
align·ment	*alnm*	al·ready	*Ar*
alive	*alv*	also	*Aso*
all	*A*	alter	*Alr*
al·le·vi·ate	*alva*	al·tera·tions	*Alrs*
alley	*Ae*	al·tered	*Alr-*
al·lied	*Ai-*	al·ter·nate	v. *Alrna* N. or adj. *Alrnt*
al·lo·cate	*Aca*	al·ter·na·tive	*Alrnv*

Word	Outline	Word	Outline
al·ter·na·tives		amounts	
al·though		ample	
alu·mi·num		amus·ing	
alumni		an	
al·ways		analy·ses	
am		analy·sis	
ama·teur		ana·lyze	
ama·teurs		ana·lyzed	
amaz·ing		ana·lyz·ing	
am·bas·sa·dor		and	
am·bi·tions		angle	
am·bu·lance		ani·mals	
amend		an·ni·ver·sary	
amended		an·nounce	
amend·ment		an·nounced	
amend·ments		an·nounce·ment	
America		an·nounce·ments	
American		an·nounc·ing	
Americans		an·noy·ance	
among		an·nual	
amount		an·nu·ally	
amounted		an·nu·ities	
amount·ing		an·nu·ity	

Word	Shorthand	Word	Shorthand
annul	*anl*	apolo·gize	*aplz*
an·other	*aol*	apology	*aplje*
an·swer	*asr*	ap·par·ent	*aprN*
an·swered	*asr-*	ap·par·ently	*aprNl*
an·swer·ing	*asr̲*	ap·peal	*apl*
an·swers	*asrs*	ap·peal·ing	*apl̲*
an·tici·pate	*alspa*	ap·peals	*apls*
an·tici·pated	*alspa-*	ap·pear	*apr*
an·tici·pa·tion	*alspj*	ap·pear·ance	*aprN*
an·tique	*alc*	ap·peared	*apr-*
anx·ious	*aqss*	ap·pear·ing	*apr̲*
any	*ne*	ap·pears	*aprs*
any·body	*nebde*	ap·pli·ance	*aplN*
any·how	*neho*	ap·pli·ances	*aplNs*
any·one	*ne1*	ap·pli·ca·ble	*aplcB*
any·thing	*ne̲*	ap·pli·cant	*aplcN*
any·time	*nel*	ap·pli·cants	*aplcNs*
any·way	*nea*	ap·pli·ca·tion	*aplcj*
any·where	*ner*	ap·pli·ca·tions	*aplcjs*
apart	*apl*	ap·plied	*apli-*
apart·ment	*aplm*	ap·plies	*aplis*
apart·ments	*aplms*	apply	*apli*
apolo·gies	*apljes*	ap·ply·ing	*apli̲*

Word	Outline	Word	Outline
ap·point	apy	ap·proved	apv-
ap·pointed	apy-	ap·proves	apvs
ap·point·ment	apym	ap·prov·ing	apv_
ap·point·ments	apyms	ap·proxi·mate	apx
ap·por·tion·ment	aprym	ap·proxi·mated	apx-
ap·praisal	aprzl	ap·proxi·mately	apxl
ap·praised	aprz-	ap·proxi·ma·tion	apxy
ap·pre·ci·ate	ap	ap·ti·tude	aplld
ap·pre·ci·ated	ap-	ar·bi·trary	arblre
ap·pre·ci·ates	aps	ar·bi·tra·tion	arblry
ap·pre·cia·tion	apy	ar·chi·tect	arclc
ap·pre·cia·tive	apv	ar·chi·tects	arclcs
ap·proach	aprC	ar·chi·tec·tural	arclcCrl
ap·proaches	aprCs	are	r
ap·proach·ing	aprC_	area	ara
ap·pro·pri·ate	apo	areas	aras
ap·pro·pri·ated	apo-	aren't	rN
ap·pro·pri·ately	apol	arena	arna
ap·pro·pri·at·ing	apo_	ar·gu·ment	argum
ap·pro·pria·tion	apoy	ar·gu·ments	argums
ap·pro·pria·tions	apojs	arise	arz
ap·proval	apvl	arises	arzs
ap·prove	apv	aris·ing	arz_

Word	Shorthand	Word	Shorthand
arm·chair	*ar⌒Cr*	arts	*arts*
army	*ar⌒e*	as	*z*
around	*aroN*	as·cer·tain	*asrtn*
ar·range	*ar*	ash	*aA*
ar·ranged	*ar-*	aside	*asd*
ar·range·ment	*arm*	ask	*asc*
ar·range·ments	*arms*	asked	*asc-*
ar·ranger	*arr*	ask·ing	*asc̲*
ar·ranges	*ars*	as·pect	*aspc*
ar·rang·ing	*ar̲*	as·pects	*aspcs*
ar·rears	*arrs*	as·phalt	*asfll*
ar·rest	*arS*	as·sem·bled	*as⌒B-*
ar·ri·val	*arvl*	as·sem·blies	*as⌒Bs*
ar·rive	*arv*	as·sem·bling	*as⌒B̲*
ar·rived	*arv-*	as·sem·bly	*as⌒B*
ar·rives	*arvs*	as·sess	*ass*
ar·riv·ing	*arv̲*	as·sessed	*ass-*
arrow	*aro*	as·sess·ment	*assm*
art	*art*	as·sess·ments	*assms*
ar·ti·cle	*artcl*	asset	*asl*
ar·ti·cles	*artcls*	as·sets	*asls*
ar·ti·fi·cial	*arlfsl*	as·sign	*asn*
art·ists	*artSs*	as·signed	*asn-*

Word	Outline	Word	Outline
as·sign·ing	*asn*	as·sured	*asr-*
as·sign·ment	*asnm*	as·sures	*asrs*
as·sign·ments	*asnms*	as·sur·ing	*asr*
as·sist	*ass*	asthma	*aza*
as·sis·tance	*assN*	asth·matic	*aztc*
as·sis·tant	*assN*	at	*,*
as·sis·tant·ship	*assNf*	ath·letic	*alltc*
as·sisted	*ass-*	atlas	*alls*
as·sist·ing	*ass*	at·mos·phere	*atsfr*
as·so·ci·ate	*aso*	atomic	*alc*
as·so·ci·ated	*aso-*	at·tach	*alC*
as·so·ci·ates	*asos*	at·tached	*alC-*
as·so·ci·at·ing	*aso*	at·taches	*alCs*
as·so·cia·tion	*asoy*	at·tach·ing	*alC*
as·so·cia·tions	*asoys*	at·tach·ment	*alCm*
as·sorted	*asrl-*	at·tack	*alc*
as·sume	*as*	at·tain·ing	*aln*
as·sumed	*as-*	at·tempt	*alt*
as·sumes	*ass*	at·tempted	*alt-*
as·sum·ing	*as*	at·tempt·ing	*alt*
as·sump·tion	*asy*	at·tempts	*alts*
as·sur·ance	*asrN*	at·tend	*alN*
as·sure	*asr*	at·ten·dance	*alNN*

Word	Shorthand	Word	Shorthand
at·tended	*alN-*	au·thor·iza·tion	*alrzɟ*
at·tend·ing	*alN_*	au·thor·ize	*alrz*
at·ten·tion	*all*	au·thor·ized	*alrz-*
at·ti·tude	*alld*	au·thor·iz·ing	*alrz_*
at·ti·tudes	*allds*	au·thors	*alrs*
at·tor·ney	*alrne*	auto	*alo*
at·tor·neys	*alrnes*	au·to·mated	*ala-*
at·tract	*alrc*	au·to·matic	*aldc*
at·tracted	*alrc-*	au·to·mat·ically	*aldcl*
at·trac·tions	*alrcɟs*	au·to·ma·tion	*alɟ*
at·trac·tive	*alrcv*	au·to·mo·bile	*aloB*
at·trib·ut·able	*alrbuB*	au·to·mo·biles	*aloBs*
au·di·ence	*adeN*	au·to·mo·tive	*alv*
audit	*adl*	aux·il·iary	*agzlre*
au·dit·ing	*adl_*	avail	*avl*
au·di·tor	*adlr*	avail·abil·ity	*avlB^l*
au·di·to·rium	*adlre*	avail·able	*avlB*
au·di·tors	*adlrs*	ave·nue	*ave*
au·dits	*adls*	ave·nues	*aves*
au·thor	*alr*	av·er·age	*avrɟ*
au·thori·ta·tive	*alrlv*	av·er·ages	*avrɟs*
au·thor·ities	*alr^ls*	av·er·ag·ing	*avrɟ_*
au·thor·ity	*alr^l*	avia·tion	*aveɟ*

avoid	*avyd*	badly	*bdl*
avoided	*avyd-*	bag	*bg*
await	*a a*	bag·gage	*bgj*
await·ing	*a a̱*	bags	*bgs*
award	*aw*	bake	*bc*
awarded	*aw-*	baked	*bc-*
awards	*aws*	bak·ery	*bcre*
aware	*a r*	bak·ing	*bc̱*
away	*a a*	bal·ance	*blN*
awe·some	*as*	bal·ances	*blNs*
axle	*l*	bale	*bl*
		bales	*bls*
B		ball	*bl*
		balls	*bls*
baby	*bbe*	bank	*bg*
back	*bc*	bank·ers	*bgrs*
backed	*bc-*	bank·ing	*bg̱*
back·ground	*bcgroN*	banks	*bgs*
back·guard	*bcgrd*	ban·ner	*bnr*
back·ing	*bc̱*	ban·quet	*bnql*
back·ward	*bcw*	bar	*br*
bad	*bd*	bar·ber	*brbr*
badges	*bjs*	bare	*br*

Word	Shorthand	Word	Shorthand
bar·gain	*brgn*	bear	*br*
bar·gain·ing	*brgn‾*	bear·ing	*br‾*
bark	*brc*	bear·ings	*br̳*
bar·rels	*brls*	bears	*brs*
bar·rier	*brer*	beat	*be*
bars	*brs*	beau·ti·ful	*blef*
base	*bs*	beau·ti·fully	*blefl*
based	*bs‾*	beauty	*ble*
base·ment	*bsm*	bea·ver	*bvr*
bases	*bss* (N. or V.) *bsz* (N.)	be·came	*bk*
basic	*bsc*	be·cause	*bcz*
ba·si·cally	*bscl*	be·come	*bk*
basin	*bsn*	be·comes	*bks*
basis	*bss*	be·com·ing	*bk‾*
batch	*bC*	bed	*bd*
bath	*bl*	bed·room	*bdr*
bat·ter·ies	*blres*	beds	*bds*
bat·tery	*blre*	beef	*bf*
bat·tle	*bll*	been	*b*
bay	*ba*	beer	*br*
be	*b*	beet	*be*
beach	*bC*	beets	*bes*
beans	*bns*	be·fore	*bf*

began	*bgn*	be·quests	*bqss*
begin	*bgn*	berths	*brts*
be·gin·ning	*bgn*	be·side	*bsd*
be·gins	*bgns*	best	*bs*
begun	*bgn*	bests	*bss*
be·half	*bhf*	bet·ter	*btr*
be·hind	*bhn*	be·tween	*btn*
being	*b*	bev·er·age	*bvrj*
be·lief	*blf*	bev·er·ages	*bvrjs*
be·lieve	*blv*	be·yond	*ben*
be·lieved	*blv-*	bib·li·og·ra·phy	*bblegrfe*
bell	*bl*	bid	*bd*
be·long·ing	*blg*	bid·der	*bdr*
below	*blo*	bid·ders	*bdrs*
belt	*bll*	bid·ding	*bd*
benches	*bnCs*	bids	*bds*
bend	*bn*	big	*bq*
bene·fi·cial	*bnfsl*	big·ger	*bgr*
bene·fi·ci·ar·ies	*bnfseres*	big·gest	*bgs*
bene·fi·ci·ary	*bnfsere*	bill	*bl*
bene·fit	*bnfl*	billed	*bl-*
bene·fits	*bnfls*	bill·ing	*bl*
be·quest	*bqs*	bil·lion	*B*

bil·lion·aire	*Br*	blind	*blm*
bil·lions	*Bs*	block	*blc*
bil·lionth	*Bl*	blocks	*blcs*
bills	*bls*	blood	*bld*
bin	*bn*	blue	*blu*
binder	*bnr*	board	*brd*
bind·ing	*bn*	boards	*brds*
bio·graph·ical	*brgrfcl*	boat	*bo*
bi·og·ra·phy	*brgrfe*	boats	*bos*
bird	*brd*	bodily	*bdl*
birds	*brds*	body	*bde*
birth	*brl*	boil	*byl*
birth·day	*brld*	boiler	*bylr*
bit	*bl*	boil·ers	*bylrs*
bite	*br*	bolts	*blls*
bits	*bls*	bond	*bn*
black	*blc*	bond·ing	*bn*
blank	*blg*	bonds	*bns*
blan·ket	*blgl*	bone	*bn*
blan·kets	*blgls*	bonus	*bns*
blanks	*blgs*	book	*bc*
bless	*bls*	booked	*bc-*
blight	*bli*	book·ings	*bc=*

Word	Outline	Word	Outline
book·keep·ing	*bccp*	bowl	*bl*
book·let	*bclt*	bowl·ing	*bl*
book·lets	*bclls*	box	*bx*
books	*bcs*	boxes	*bxs*
boom	*b*	boy	*by*
booth	*bl*	boy·hood	*byh*
booths	*bls*	boys	*bys*
bor·der	*brdr*	branch	*brnc*
bore	*br*	branches	*brncs*
born	*brn*	brand	*brn*
borne	*brn*	bread	*brd*
bor·row	*bro*	break	*brc*
bor·rowed	*bro-*	break·age	*brcy*
both	*bo*	break·down	*brcdon*
bot·tle	*bll*	break·fast	*brcfs*
bot·tles	*blls*	break·ing	*brc*
bot·tom	*bl*	breaks	*brcs*
bought	*bl*	breeder	*brdr*
boule·vard	*blvd*	brew·ing	*bru*
boule·vards	*blvds*	brick	*brc*
bound	*boN*	bridge	*by*
bounda·ries	*boNres*	bridges	*bys*
bow	*bo*	brief	*brf*

briefly	*brfl*	budg·eted	*bjt-*
bright	*bri*	budg·ets	*bjts*
bring	*brg*	build	*bld*
bring·ing	*brg-*	build·ers	*bldrs*
brings	*brgs*	build·ing	*bld*
broad	*brd*	build·ings	*bld*
broad·cast	*brdcs*	built	*blt*
broader	*brdr*	bulbs	*blbs*
bro·chure	*brsr*	bulk	*blc*
bro·chures	*brsrs*	bul·le·tin	*blln*
bro·ken	*brcn*	bul·le·tins	*bllns*
bro·ker	*brcr*	bur·den	*brdn*
bro·kers	*brcrs*	bu·reau	*bro*
brother	*brtr*	bu·reaus	*bros*
broth·ers	*brtrs*	burned	*brn-*
brought	*brt*	burner	*brnr*
brown	*bron*	bus	*bs*
browse	*broz*	busi·ness	*bs*
brush	*brs*	busi·nesses	*bss*
bucket	*bct*	busi·ness·like	*bslc*
buck·ets	*bcts*	busi·ness·man	*bs_m*
bud	*bd*	busi·ness·men	*bsm*
budget	*bjt*	busi·ness·woman	*bs_m*

Word	Outline
busi·ness·women	*bs m*
busy	*bze*
but	*b*
but·ler	*bllr*
but·ton	*bln*
but·tons	*blns*
buy	*b*
buyer	*br*
buy·ers	*brs*
buy·ing	*b_*
buys	*bs*
by	*b*
by·laws	*blas*
by·pass	*bps*

C

Word	Outline
cabi·net	*cbnl*
cabi·nets	*cbnls*
cable	*cB*
ca·ble·gram	*cBg*
cafe·te·ria	*cflra*
cake	*cc*

Word	Outline
cakes	*ccs*
cal·cu·late	*clcla*
cal·cu·lated	*clcla-*
cal·cu·lat·ing	*clcla_*
cal·cu·la·tion	*clclj*
cal·cu·la·tor	*clclar*
cal·en·dar	*clNr*
call	*cl*
called	*cl-*
call·ing	*cl_*
calls	*cls*
came	*k*
cam·era	*c ra*
camp	*c p*
cam·paign	*c pn*
camp·ing	*c p_*
cam·pus	*c ps*
can	*c*
can't	*cM*
Canadian	*cnden*
canal	*cnl*
can·cel	*csl*
can·celed	*csl-*

Word	Outline	Word	Outline
can·cel·ing	*csl̄*	cap·ture	*cpcr*
can·cel·la·tion	*csly*	car	*cr*
can·cel·la·tions	*cslys*	car·bon	*crbn*
can·cer	*csr*	card	*crd*
can·did	*cdd*	card·board	*crdbrd*
can·di·date	*cddt cdda*	car·diac	*crdec*
can·di·dates	*cddts*	cards	*crds*
candy	*cde*	care	*cr*
cane	*cn*	ca·reer	*crr*
canned	*c-*	ca·reers	*crrs*
can·not	*cn*	care·ful	*crf*
cans	*cs*	care·fully	*crfl*
cap	*cp*	care·less·ness	*crls'*
ca·pa·bil·ities	*cpℬ ls*	cargo	*crg*
ca·pa·bil·ity	*cpℬ l*	car·load	*crld*
ca·pa·ble	*cpℬ*	car·pet	*crpt*
ca·pac·ity	*cps l*	car·pet·ing	*crpt̄*
capi·tal	*cptl*	car·port	*crpt*
capi·tol	*cptl*	car·ried	*cre-*
cap·tain	*cptn*	car·rier	*crer*
cap·tion	*cpy*	car·ri·ers	*crers*
cap·tioned	*cpy-*	car·ries	*cres*
cap·tions	*cpys*	carry	*cre*

Word	Outline	Word	Outline
car·ry·ing	*cre*	caused	*cz-*
cars	*crs*	causes	*czs*
car·ton	*crtn*	caus·ing	*cz*
car·tons	*crtns*	ceil·ing	*slg*
car·toons	*crtns*	cele·bra·tion	*slbry*
case	*cs*	cell	*sl*
cases	*css*	Celsius	*slses*
cash	*cA*	ce·ment	*sm*
cashed	*cA-*	ceme·tery	*smre*
cash·iers	*cArs*	cen·sus	*sns*
cas·ing	*cs*	cent	*¢*
cast	*cs*	cen·ter	*snr*
casual	*czul*	cen·ters	*snrs*
casu·alty	*czulle*	cen·tral	*snrl*
cata·log	*cal*	cen·tral·ized	*snrlz-*
cata·logs	*cals*	cen·trifu·gal	*sntrfgl*
catch	*cC*	cents	*¢*
cate·go·ries	*clgres*	cen·tury	*sncre*
cate·gory	*clgre*	cer·tain	*Stn*
cat·er·pil·lar	*clrplr*	cer·tainly	*Stnl*
cat·tle	*cll*	cer·tifi·cate	*Stfcl*
caught	*cl*	cer·tifi·cates	*Stfcls*
cause	*cz*	cer·ti·fi·ca·tion	*Stff*

Word	Outline	Word	Outline
cer·ti·fied	_Slf-_	chapel	_Cpl_
cer·tify	_Slf_	chap·ter	_Cplr_
chain	_Cn_	chap·ters	_Cplrs_
chair	_Cr_	char·ac·ter	_crc_
chair·man	_Crm_	char·ac·ter·is·tic	_crc_
chair·men	_Crm_	char·ac·ter·is·ti·cally	_crcl_
chair·per·son	_CrPsn_	char·ac·ter·is·tics	_crcs_
chairs	_Crs_	char·ac·ter·iza·tion	_crcz_
chair·woman	_Crm_	char·ac·ter·iza·tions	_crczs_
chair·women	_Crm_	char·ac·ter·ize	_crcz_
chal·lenge	_Clng_	char·ac·ter·iz·ing	_crcz-_
chal·lenges	_Clnjs_	char·ac·ters	_crcs_
chal·leng·ing	_Clng-_	charge	_G_
cham·ber	_Cbr_	charged	_G-_
cham·bers	_Cbrs_	charges	_Gs_
chance	_CN_	charg·ing	_G-_
chances	_CNs_	chari·ta·ble	_CrlB_
change	_Cnj_	chart	_Crl_
changed	_Cnj-_	char·ter	_Crlr_
changes	_Cnjs_	charts	_Crls_
chang·ing	_Cnj-_	chase	_Cs_
chan·nel	_Cnl_	cheaper	_Cpr_
chan·nels	_Cnls_	check	_Cc_

Word	Shorthand	Word	Shorthand
checked	*Cc-*	church	*CrC*
check·ing	*Cc_*	churches	*CrCs*
checks	*Ccs*	ciga·rette	*sgrt*
chem·ical	*crcl*	cir·cle	*Scl*
chem·icals	*crcls*	cir·cuit	*Scl*
chem·is·try	*cSre*	cir·cuits	*Scls*
cherry	*Cre*	cir·cu·lar	*Sclr*
chest	*CS*	cir·cu·lat·ing	*Scla_*
chief	*Cf*	cir·cu·la·tion	*Sclf*
child	*Cld*	cir·cum·stance	*Sk*
child·hood	*Cldh*	cir·cum·stances	*Sks*
chil·dren	*Cldrn*	cir·cum·stan·tial	*SkSl*
chilled	*Cl-*	cite	*st*
chips	*Cps*	cit·ies	*stes*
choco·late	*Cclt*	citi·zen	*stzn*
choice	*Cys*	citi·zens	*stzns*
choices	*Cyss*	cit·rus	*strs*
choose	*Cz*	city	*ste*
choos·ing	*Cz_*	civic	*svc*
chose	*Cz*	civil	*svl*
cho·sen	*Czn*	ci·vil·ian	*svlyn*
Christmas	*Xs*	ci·vil·ians	*svlyns*
Christmases	*Xss*	civi·li·za·tion	*svlzy*

claim	*cl*	clear	*clr*
claim·ant	*clM*	clear·ance	*clrN*
claimed	*cl-*	cleared	*clr-*
claim·ing	*cl_*	clear·ing	*clr_*
claims	*cls*	clearly	*clrl*
clari·fi·ca·tion	*clrff*	cler·ical	*clrcl*
clari·fied	*clrf-*	clerk	*clrc*
clarify	*clrf*	clerks	*clrcs*
clari·fy·ing	*clrf_*	clever	*clvr*
class	*cls*	cli·ent	*clM*
classes	*clss*	cli·ents	*clMs*
clas·si·fi·ca·tion	*clsff*	cli·mate	*cll*
clas·si·fi·ca·tions	*clsffs*	clinic	*clnc*
clas·si·fied	*clsf-*	clin·ical	*clncl*
class·room	*clsr*	clock	*clc*
class·rooms	*clsrs*	close	*cls* adj. *clz* v.
clause	*clz*	closed	*clz-*
clay	*cla*	closely	*clsl*
clean	*cln*	closer	*clsr*
cleaned	*cln-*	closes	*clzs*
cleaner	*clnr*	closet	*clzt*
clean·ers	*clnrs*	clos·ing	*clz_*
clean·ing	*cln_*	cloth	*cll*

cloth·ing	*cll*	col·lect	*clc*
club	*clb*	col·lected	*clc-*
clubs	*clbs*	col·lect·ing	*clc*
clus·ter	*clSr*	col·lec·tion	*clcy*
coach	*cc*	col·lec·tions	*clcys*
coal	*cl*	col·lec·tively	*clcvl*
coast	*cS*	col·lege	*cly*
coat	*co*	col·leges	*clys*
coated	*co-*	col·li·sion	*cly*
coat·ing	*co*	color	*clr*
coat·ings	*co*	col·or·ful	*clrf*
coats	*cos*	col·ors	*clrs*
coat·tail	*coll*	col·umn	*ch*
code	*cd*	col·umns	*chs*
coded	*cd-*	com·bi·na·tion	*kbny*
codes	*cds*	com·bi·na·tions	*kbnys*
cod·ing	*cd*	com·bine	*kbn*
cof·fee	*cfe*	com·bined	*kbn-*
coil	*cyl*	come	*k*
cold	*cld*	comes	*ks*
col·lat·eral	*cllrl*	com·fort	*kfl*
col·league	*clq*	com·fort·able	*kflB*
col·leagues	*clqs*	com·ing	*k*

com·mand	*kN*	com·mod·ity	*kdˡ*
com·mence	*kN*	com·mon	*kn*
com·mence·ment	*kNm*	com·mon·wealth	*kn ll*
com·menc·ing	*kN*	com·mu·ni·cate	*knca*
com·mend	*kN*	com·mu·ni·ca·tion	*kncy*
com·men·su·rate	*kNrl*	com·mu·ni·ca·tions	*kncys*
com·ment	*kN*	com·mu·ni·ties	*kn ˡᵒ*
com·mented	*kN-*	com·mu·nity	*kn ˡ*
com·ment·ing	*kN*	com·pact	*kpc*
com·ments	*kNs*	com·pa·nies	*cos*
com·merce	*krs*	com·pan·ion	*kpnyn*
com·mer·cial	*krsl*	com·pan·ion·ship	*kpnyns*
com·mer·cials	*krsls*	com·pany	*co*
com·mis·sion	*kj*	com·pa·ra·ble	*kprß*
com·mis·sioner	*kjr*	com·para·tive	*kprv*
com·mis·sion·ers	*kjrs*	com·pare	*kpr*
com·mis·sions	*kjs*	com·pared	*kpr-*
com·mit·ment	*klm*	com·pari·son	*kprsn*
com·mit·ments	*klms*	com·part·ment	*kplm*
com·mit·ted	*kl-*	com·part·ments	*kplms*
com·mit·tee	*k*	com·pat·ible	*kplß*
com·mit·tees	*ks*	com·pen·sate	*kpNa*
com·mod·ities	*kd ˡᵒ*	com·pen·sa·tion	*kpNy*

com·pete	*kpe*	com·pli·men·tary	*kplmre*
com·pe·tent	*kplN*	com·pli·ments	*kplms*
com·pe·ti·tion	*kply*	com·ply	*kpli*
com·peti·tive	*kplv*	com·ply·ing	*kpli*
com·pile	*kpl*	com·po·nents	*kpnNs*
com·piled	*kpl-*	com·posed	*kpz-*
com·pil·ing	*kpl*	com·pounded	*kpoN-*
com·plain	*kpln*	com·pre·hen·sive	*kprhNv*
com·plaint	*kplN*	com·pres·sor	*kprsr*
com·plaints	*kplNs*	com·pres·sors	*kprsrs*
com·ple·ment	*kplm*	com·pro·mise	*kprz*
com·plete	*kp*	comp·trol·ler	*klr*
com·pleted	*kp-*	com·pu·ta·tion	*kply*
com·pletely	*kpl*	com·pu·ta·tions	*kplys*
com·plete·ness	*kp'*	com·pute	*kpu*
com·pletes	*kps*	com·puted	*kpu-*
com·plet·ing	*kp*	com·puter	*kpur*
com·ple·tion	*kpy*	com·put·ers	*kpurs*
com·plex	*kplx*	com·put·ing	*kpu*
com·pli·ance	*kplN*	con·ceal	*ksl*
com·pli·cated	*kplca-*	con·cealed	*ksl-*
com·plied	*kpli-*	con·ceiv·able	*ksv8*
com·pli·ment	*kplm*	con·cen·trated	*ksNra-*

con·cept	*kspl*	con·duct	*kdc*
con·cepts	*kspls*	con·ducted	*kdc-*
con·cern	*ksrn*	con·duct·ing	*kdc̲*
con·cerned	*ksrn-*	con·duc·tor	*kdcr*
con·cern·ing	*ksrn̲*	con·fer·ence	*kfrN*
con·cerns	*ksrns*	con·fer·ences	*kfrNs*
con·certed	*ksrt-*	con·ferred	*kfr-*
con·ces·sion	*ksy*	con·fi·dence	*kfdN*
con·ces·sions	*ksys*	con·fi·dent	*kfdN*
con·clude	*kcld*	con·fi·den·tial	*kfdnsl*
con·cluded	*kcld-*	con·fi·dently	*kfdNl*
con·clu·sion	*kcly*	con·fined	*kfn-*
con·clu·sions	*kclys*	con·fine·ment	*kfnm*
con·crete	*kcre*	con·firm	*kfr*
con·cur	*kcr*	con·fir·ma·tion	*kfry*
con·cur·rence	*kcrN*	con·firmed	*kfr-*
con·cur·ring	*kcr̲*	con·firm·ing	*kfr̲*
con·densed	*kdN-*	con·firms	*kfrs*
con·denser	*kdNr*	con·flict	*kflc*
con·di·tion	*kdy*	con·flicts	*kflcs*
con·di·tional	*kdyl*	con·form	*kf*
con·di·tion·ing	*kdy̲*	con·formed	*kf-*
con·di·tions	*kdys*	con·form·ing	*kf̲*

Word	Outline	Word	Outline
con·forms	*kfs*	con·ser·va·tive	*ksrvv*
con·fuse	*kfz*	con·sider	*ks*
con·fused	*kfz-*	con·sid·er·able	*ksB*
con·fus·ing	*kfz_*	con·sid·er·ably	*ksB*
con·fu·sion	*kfj*	con·sid·er·ate	*ksl*
con·ges·tion	*kjsj*	con·sid·era·tion	*ksj*
con·gratu·late	*kq*	con·sid·era·tions	*ksjs*
con·gratu·la·tions	*kgjs*	con·sid·ered	*ks-*
con·gress	*kgrs*	con·sid·er·ing	*ks_*
con·gres·sional	*kgrjl*	con·sid·ers	*kss*
con·gress·man	*kgrs~m*	con·signee	*ksne*
con·gress·wom·an	*kgrs~m*	con·sist	*ksS*
con·junc·tion	*kjqj*	con·sisted	*ksS-*
con·nect	*kc*	con·sis·tent	*ksSN*
con·nected	*kc-*	con·sis·tently	*ksSNl*
con·nec·tion	*kcj*	con·sist·ing	*ksS_*
con·nec·tions	*kcjs*	con·sists	*ksSs*
con·scious·ness	*kss'*	con·soli·dated	*kslda-*
con·sen·sus	*ksNs*	con·stant	*kSN*
con·sent	*ksN*	con·stantly	*kSNl*
con·se·quence	*ksqN*	con·stitu·ent	*kSCuN*
con·se·quently	*ksqNl*	con·sti·tute	*kSlu*
con·ser·va·tion	*ksrvj*	con·sti·tutes	*kSlus*

Word	Outline	Word	Outline
con·sti·tu·tion	kSy	con·tainer	ktnr
con·sti·tu·tional	kSyl	con·tain·ers	ktnrs
con·struct	kSrc	con·tain·ing	ktn_
con·structed	kSrc-	con·tains	ktns
con·struct·ing	kSrc_	con·tami·na·tion	ktmy
con·struc·tion	kSrcy	con·tem·plate	kt–pla
con·struc·tive	kSrcv	con·tem·plated	kt–pla-
con·sult	ksll	con·tem·plat·ing	kt–pla_
con·sult·ant	ksllN	con·tem·po·rary	kt–prre
con·sult·ants	ksllNs	con·tent	ktN
con·sul·ta·tion	kslly	con·tents	ktNs
con·sulted	ksll-	con·test	ktS
con·sult·ing	ksll_	con·tests	ktSs
con·sumer	ks–r	con·ti·nen·tal	ktnNl
con·sum·ers	ks–rs	con·tin·gent	ktnyN
con·sum·mate	ks–a _v._ ks–t _adj._	con·tinual	kul
con·sump·tion	ks–y	con·tinu·ally	kull
con·tact	ktc	con·tinu·ation	kuy
con·tacted	ktc-	con·tinue	ku
con·tact·ing	ktc_	con·tin·ued	ku-
con·tacts	ktcs	con·tin·ues	kus
con·tain	ktn	con·tinu·ing	ku_
con·tained	ktn-	con·ti·nu·ity	ku'

con·tinu·ous	*kus*	con·trol·lers	*klrs*
con·tinu·ously	*kusl*	con·trol·ling	*kl*
con·tinuum	*ku*	con·trols	*kls*
con·tract	*kc*	con·tro·ver·sial	*klrvrsl*
con·tracted	*kc-*	con·ven·ience	*kv*
con·tract·ing	*kc*	con·ven·iences	*kvs*
con·trac·tor	*kcr*	con·ven·ient	*kv*
con·trac·tors	*kcrs*	con·ven·iently	*kvl*
con·tracts	*kcs*	con·ven·tion	*kvny*
con·trac·tual	*kcul*	con·ven·tional	*kvnyl*
con·trary	*klrre*	con·ven·tions	*kvnys*
con·trib·ute	*kb*	con·ver·sa·tion	*kvrsy*
con·trib·uted	*kb-*	con·ver·sa·tions	*kvrsys*
con·trib·utes	*kbs*	con·ver·sion	*kvry*
con·trib·ut·ing	*kb*	con·vert	*kvrl*
con·tri·bu·tion	*kby*	con·verted	*kvrl -*
con·tri·bu·tions	*kbys*	con·vert·ible	*kvrlB*
con·tribu·tor	*kbr*	con·vert·ing	*kvrl*
con·tribu·tors	*kbrs*	con·vey	*kva*
con·tribu·tory	*kbre*	con·vey·ance	*kvaN*
con·trol	*kl*	con·veyor	*kvar*
con·trolled	*kl-*	con·vic·tion	*kvcy*
con·trol·ler	*klr*	con·vince	*kvN*

Word	Outline	Word	Outline
con·vinced	*kvN-*	cor·dially	*cryll*
cook	*cc*	core	*cr*
cook·ing	*cc_*	corn	*crn*
cool·ers	*clrs*	cor·ner	*crnr*
cool·ing	*cl_*	cor·ners	*crnrs*
co·op·er·ate	*cop*	cor·po·rate	*crprt*
co·op·er·ated	*cop-*	cor·po·ra·tion	*corp*
co·op·er·ates	*cops*	cor·po·ra·tions	*corps*
co·op·er·at·ing	*cop_*	corps	*cr*
co·op·era·tion	*copy*	cor·rect	*crc*
co·op·era·tive	*copv*	cor·rected	*crc-*
co·op·era·tively	*copvl*	cor·rec·tion	*crcy*
co·op·era·tives	*copvs*	cor·rec·tional	*crcyl*
co·or·di·nate	*cordna* (v.) *cordnt* (adj. or N.)	cor·rec·tions	*crcys*
co·or·di·nated	*cordna-*	cor·rec·tive	*crcv*
co·or·di·na·tion	*cordny*	cor·rectly	*crcl*
co·or·di·na·tor	*cordnar*	cor·re·spond	*cor*
copier	*cper*	cor·re·sponded	*cor-*
cop·ies	*cpes*	cor·re·spon·dence	*cor*
cop·per	*cpr*	cor·re·spon·dent	*corN*
copy	*cpe*	cor·re·spon·dents	*corNs*
copy·ing	*cpe_*	cor·re·spond·ing	*cor_*
cor·dial	*cryl*	cor·re·sponds	*cors*

Word	Shorthand	Word	Shorthand
cor·ro·sion	cry	cou·ple	cpl
cost	cS	cou·ples	cpls
cost·ing	cS	cou·pon	cpn
costly	cSl	cou·pons	cpns
costs	cSs	course	crs
cot·ton	cln	courses	crss
could	cd	court	crl
couldn't	cdN	cour·te·sies	crlses
coun·cil	ksl	cour·tesy	crlse
coun·sel	ksl	courts	crls
coun·sel·ing	ksl	cover	cvr
coun·selor	kslr	cov·er·age	cvry
coun·sel·ors	kslrs	cov·er·ages	cvrys
count	k	cov·ered	cvr -
counter	kr	cov·er·ing	cvr
coun·ter·part	krpl	cov·ers	cvrs
count·ers	krs	cracked	crc -
coun·ties	kes	crafts	crfls
count·ing	k	cre·ate	cra
count·less	kls	cre·ated	cra-
coun·tries	cNres	cre·ates	cras
coun·try	cNre	cre·at·ing	cra
county	ke	crea·tive	crav

Word	Shorthand	Word	Shorthand
cre·den·tials	*crdnsls*	crys·tal	*crSl*
credit	*cr*	cubic	*cbc*
cred·it·able	*crB*	cues	*cus*
cred·ited	*cr -*	cuffs	*cfs*
cred·it·ing	*cr̲*	cul·tural	*clCrl*
credi·tor	*crr*	cul·ture	*clCr*
credi·tors	*crrs*	curb	*crb*
cred·its	*crs*	cure	*cr*
creek	*crc*	cured	*cr -*
crew	*cru*	cur·ing	*cr̲*
crews	*crus*	cu·ri·ous	*cres*
crip·pled	*crpl-*	cur·ren·cies	*crNes*
cri·sis	*crss*	cur·rency	*crNe*
cri·te·ria	*crlra*	cur·rent	*crN*
crit·ical	*crlcl*	cur·rently	*crNl*
crit·ics	*crlcs*	cur·ricu·lum	*crcl*
crop	*crp*	cus·tom	*cS*
crops	*crps*	cus·tom·arily	*cSrl*
cross	*crs*	cus·tomer	*K*
crossed	*crs -*	cus·tom·ers	*Ks*
cross·ing	*crs̲*	cus·toms	*cSs*
crude	*crd*	cut	*cl*
cru·sade	*crsd*	cute	*cu*

Word	Outline	Word	Outline
cut·ting	*cl*	dates	*das*
cycle	*scl*	daugh·ter	*dlr*
cy·cles	*scls*	daugh·ters	*dlrs*
cyl·in·der	*slNr*	day	*d*
cyl·in·ders	*slNrs*	day·break	*dbrc*
		day·dream	*ddr*
D		day·light	*dli*
		days	*ds*
dai·lies	*dls*	day·time	*dl*
daily	*dl*	dead	*dd*
dairy	*dre*	dead·line	*ddln*
dam·age	*dry*	deaf	*df*
dam·aged	*dry-*	deal	*dl*
dam·ages	*drys*	dealer	*dlr*
dance	*dN*	deal·ers	*dlrs*
dan·ger	*dnyr*	deal·ing	*dl*
dan·ger·ous	*dnyrs*	deal·ings	*dl*
dan·gers	*dnyrs*	deals	*dls*
dark	*drc*	dealt	*dll*
dar·ling	*drlg*	dean	*dn*
data	*dla*	death	*dl*
date	*da*	de·bate	*dba*
dated	*da-*	de·ben·tures	*dbnCrs*

debts	*dls*	de·duct·ing	*ddc*
dec·ade	*dcd*	de·duc·tion	*ddcy*
de·ceased	*dss-*	de·duc·tions	*ddcys*
de·cide	*dsd*	deed	*dd*
de·cided	*dsd-*	deemed	*d~-*
de·ci·sion	*dsy*	deep	*dp*
de·ci·sions	*dsys*	deep·est	*dp8*
de·ci·sive	*dssv*	deeply	*dpl*
deck	*dc*	de·fect	*dfc*
decks	*dcs*	de·fec·tive	*dfcv*
dec·la·ra·tion	*dclry*	de·fects	*dfcs*
dec·la·ra·tions	*dclrys*	de·fen·dant	*dfNN*
de·clared	*dclr-*	de·fen·dants	*dfNNs*
de·cline	*dcln*	de·fense	*dfN*
de·clined	*dcln-*	defer	*dfr*
deco·rat·ing	*dcra*	de·fer·ment	*dfrm*
de·crease	*dcrs*	de·ferred	*dfr-*
de·creased	*dcrs-*	defi·cit	*dfst*
dedi·cated	*ddca-*	de·fine	*dfn*
dedi·ca·tion	*ddcy*	de·fined	*dfn-*
de·duct	*ddc*	defi·nite	*dfnt*
de·ducted	*ddc-*	defi·nitely	*dfntl*
de·duct·ible	*ddc8*	defi·ni·tion	*dfny*

de·gree	*dgre*	de·luxe	*dlx*
delay	*dla*	de·mand	*dm*
de·layed	*dla-*	de·mand·ing	*dm*
de·lays	*dlas*	de·mands	*dms*
dele·gate	*dlgă dlğl*	dem·on·strate	*dmSra*
dele·gated	*dlga-*	dem·on·strated	*dmSra-*
dele·gates	*dlgăs dlğls*	dem·on·strates	*dmSras*
de·lete	*dle*	dem·on·stra·tion	*dmSrj*
de·leted	*dle-*	dem·on·stra·tions	*dmSrjs*
de·le·tion	*dlj*	de·nial	*dnil*
de·light	*dli*	de·nied	*dni-*
de·lighted	*dli-*	den·sity	*dNᴸ*
de·light·ful	*dlif*	den·tal	*dNl*
de·lin·quency	*dlq Ne*	deny	*dni*
de·lin·quent	*dlq N*	de·part	*dpl*
de·liver	*dl*	de·part·ment	*dpl*
de·liv·er·ance	*dlN*	de·part·men·tal	*dpll*
de·liv·ered	*dl-*	de·part·men·tal·iza·tion	*dpllzj*
de·liv·er·ies	*dles*	de·part·men·tal·ize	*dpllz*
de·liv·er·ing	*dl*	de·part·men·tal·izes	*dpllzs*
de·liv·ers	*dls*	de·part·ments	*dpls*
de·liv·ery	*dle*	de·parts	*dpls*
delta	*dlla*	de·par·ture	*dplr*

Word	Shorthand	Word	Shorthand
de·pend	dpN	deputy	dple
de·pend·able	dpNB	de·rided	drd-
de·pend·ent	dpNN	de·rived	drv-
de·pend·ents	dpNNs	de·scribe	dS
de·pend·ing	dpN̲	de·scribed	dS-
de·pends	dpNs	de·scribes	dSs
de·pleted	dple-	de·scrib·ing	dS̲
de·port	dpl	de·scrip·tion	dSy
de·por·ta·tion	dply	de·scrip·tions	dSys
de·por·ta·tions	dplys	de·scrip·tive	dSv
de·ported	dpl-	de·serve	dzrv
de·port·ing	dpl̲	de·serves	dzrvs
de·port·ment	dplm	de·serv·ing	dzrv̲
de·ports	dpls	de·sign	dzn
de·posit	dpzl	des·ig·nate (v.) dzḡna (adj.) dzḡnl	
de·pos·ited	dpzl-	des·ig·nated	dzgna-
depo·si·tion	dpzy	des·ig·nat·ing	dzgna̲
de·pos·its	dpzls	des·ig·na·tion	dzgny
depot	dpo	de·signed	dzn-
de·pre·cia·tion	dprsey	de·signs	dzns
de·pres·sion	dpry	de·sir·able	dzrB
dep·ri·va·tion	dprvy	de·sire	dzr
depth	dpl̲	de·sired	dzr-

Word	Shorthand	Word	Shorthand
de·sires	*dzrs*	de·vel·op·ers	*dvrs*
de·sir·ous	*dzrs*	de·vel·op·ing	*dv_*
desk	*dsc*	de·vel·op·ment	*dvm*
desks	*dscs*	de·vel·op·mental	*dvml*
de·spite	*dspi*	de·vel·op·ment·ally	*dvmll*
des·ti·na·tion	*dSny*	de·vel·op·ments	*dvms*
de·stroy	*dSry*	de·vel·ops	*dvs*
de·stroyed	*dSry-*	de·vice	*dvo*
de·tail	*dll*	de·vices	*dvss*
de·tailed	*dll-*	de·vise	*dvz*
de·tails	*dlls*	de·vises	*dvzs*
de·tect	*dlc*	de·vote	*dvo*
de·tec·tion	*dlcy*	de·voted	*dvo-*
de·ter·gent	*dlrjN*	dia·be·tes	*dibls*
de·te·rio·ra·tion	*dlrery*	di·ag·no·sis	*dignss*
de·ter·mi·na·tion	*dly*	dia·gram	*dig*
de·ter·mine	*dl*	dial	*dil*
de·ter·mined	*dl-*	di·ame·ter	*di~lr*
de·ter·mines	*dls*	dia·mond	*dmd*
de·ter·min·ing	*dl_*	dic·tat·ing	*dcla_*
de·velop	*dv*	dic·ta·tion	*dcly*
de·vel·oped	*dv-*	dic·tion·ary	*dcyre*
de·vel·oper	*dvr*	did	*dd*

Word	Outline	Word	Outline
didn't	*ddN*	di·rec·tion	*dry*
die	*di*	di·rec·tions	*drys*
died	*di-*	di·rec·tive	*drv*
dies	*dis*	di·rec·tives	*drvs*
die·sel	*dsl*	di·rectly	*drl*
diet	*dil*	di·rec·tor	*drr*
dif·fer·ence	*dfrN*	di·rec·to·ries	*drres*
dif·fer·ences	*dfrNs*	di·rec·tors	*drrs*
dif·fer·ent	*dfrN*	di·rec·tory	*drre*
dif·fi·cult	*dfc*	dis·abil·ity	*DBl*
dif·fi·cul·ties	*dfces*	dis·abled	*DB-*
dif·fi·culty	*dfce*	dis·ad·van·tage	*DAv*
di·gest	*djS*	dis·ap·pear	*Dapr*
dili·gent	*dljN*	dis·ap·pear·ance	*DaprN*
dili·gently	*dljNl*	dis·ap·point	*Dapy*
di·men·sions	*dmjs*	dis·ap·pointed	*Dapy-*
din·ing	*dn_*	dis·ap·point·ment	*Dapym*
din·ner	*dnr*	dis·ap·proval	*Dapvl*
di·ploma	*dpl~a*	dis·ap·prove	*Dapv*
di·plo·mas	*dpl~as*	dis·ap·proved	*Dapv-*
di·rect	*dr*	dis·ap·proves	*Dapvs*
di·rected	*dr-*	dis·ap·prov·ing	*Dapv_*
di·rect·ing	*dr_*	dis·as·ter	*dzSr*

disc	*Dc*	dis·eases	*dzzs*
dis·charge	*Dcy*	dis·may	*Dra*
dis·charged	*Dcy-*	dis·or·gan·iza·tion	*Dogy*
dis·charg·ing	*Dcy_*	dis·or·gan·ize	*Doq*
dis·close	*Dclz*	dis·or·gan·ized	*Doq-*
dis·closes	*Dclzs*	dis·patcher	*Dpcr*
dis·clo·sure	*Dclzr*	dis·play	*Dpla*
dis·com·fort	*Dkfl*	dis·played	*Dpla-*
dis·con·tinue	*Dku*	dis·play·ing	*Dpla_*
dis·con·tin·ued	*Dku-*	dis·plays	*Dplas*
dis·con·tinu·ing	*Dku_*	dis·please	*Dp*
dis·count	*Dk*	dis·pleased	*Dp-*
dis·counts	*Dks*	dis·pleases	*Dps*
dis·cover	*Dcvr*	dis·posal	*Dpzl*
dis·cov·ered	*Dcvr-*	dis·pose	*Dpz*
dis·cre·tion	*Dcry*	dis·posed	*Dpz-*
dis·cuss	*Dcs*	dis·pos·ing	*Dpz_*
dis·cussed	*Dcs-*	dis·po·si·tion	*Dpzy*
dis·cusses	*Dcss*	dis·prove	*Dpv*
dis·cuss·ing	*Dcs_*	dis·proved	*Dpv-*
dis·cus·sion	*Dcy*	dis·proves	*Dpvs*
dis·cus·sions	*Dcys*	dis·pute	*Dpu*
dis·ease	*dzz*	dis·re·gard	*Dre*

Word	Shorthand	Word	Shorthand
dis·sat·is·fac·tion		di·ver·si·fi·ca·tion	
dis·tance		di·vided	
dis·tinct		divi·dend	
dis·tinc·tive		divi·dends	
dis·tin·guish		di·vides	
dis·tin·guished		di·vid·ing	
dis·trib·ute		di·vi·sion	
dis·trib·uted		di·vi·sions	
dis·trib·utes		do	
dis·trib·ut·ing		dock	
dis·tri·bu·tion		docket	
dis·tri·bu·tions		doc·tor	
dis·tribu·tive		doc·toral	
dis·tribu·tor		doc·tor·ate	
dis·tribu·tors		doc·tored	
dis·tribu·tor·ship		doc·tor·ing	
dis·trict		doc·tors	
dis·tricts		docu·ment	
dis·turb		docu·ments	
dis·turbed		does	
ditch		doesn't	
ditches		dog	
ditto		doing	

dol·lar	$	drain	*drn*
dol·lars	$	drain·age	*drnj*
do·mes·tic	*d Sc*	drama	*dr a*
don't	*dN*	dra·matic	*dr Sc*
do·nated	*dna-*	draw	*dra*
do·na·tion	*dnj*	draw·ing	*dra_*
done	*dn*	draw·ings	*dra=*
donor	*dnr*	drawn	*drn*
door	*dr*	dress	*drs*
doors	*drs*	dress·ing	*drs_*
dose	*ds*	drill	*drl*
dou·ble	*dB*	drilled	*drl-*
dou·bled	*dB-*	drill·ing	*drl_*
doubt	*dol*	drills	*drls*
doubted	*dol-*	drinks	*drqs*
doubt·ful	*dolf*	drive	*drv*
down	*don*	driven	*drvn*
down·hill	*donhl*	driver	*drvr*
down·town	*donton*	driv·ers	*drvrs*
down·ward	*donw*	driv·ing	*drv_*
dozen	*dzn*	drop	*drp*
draft	*drfl*	dropped	*drp-*
drafts	*drfls*	drop·ping	*drp_*

Word	Shorthand	Word	Shorthand
drops	*drps*		**E**
drug	*drg*		
drums	*dr—s*	each	*eC*
dry	*dri*	eager	*egr*
dual	*dul*	ear	*er*
ducts	*dcs*	ear·lier	*erlr*
due	*du*	ear·li·est	*erlS*
dues	*dus*	early	*erl*
duly	*dul*	earn	*ern*
dump	*d—p*	earned	*ern-*
dun	*dn*	ear·nestly	*ernSl*
du·pli·cate	*dplcl* adj. *dplca* v.	earn·ing	*ern_*
du·pli·cated	*dplca-*	earn·ings	*ern=*
du·pli·cat·ing	*dplca_*	earth	*erl*
du·pli·ca·tion	*dplcj*	ease	*ez*
du·pli·ca·tors	*dplcars*	ease·ment	*ezm*
du·ra·ble	*drB*	easier	*ezer*
du·ra·tion	*dry*	easily	*ezl*
dur·ing	*du_*	east	*E*
du·ties	*dles*	east·erly	*Erl*
duty	*dle*	east·ern	*Ern*
dwell·ing	*dl_*	east·ward	*Ew*
dy·namic	*dn—c*	easy	*eze*

eat	*el*	ef·fec·tive	*efcv*
eco·nomic	*eco*	ef·fec·tively	*efcvl*
eco·nom·ical	*ecol*	ef·fec·tive·ness	*efcv'*
eco·nom·ically	*ecoll*	ef·fects	*efcs*
eco·nom·ics	*ecos*	ef·fi·ciency	*efʌne*
econo·mies	*ecos*	ef·fi·cient	*efʌn*
econo·mist	*ecoʃ*	ef·fi·ciently	*efʌnl*
econo·mists	*ecoʃs*	ef·fort	*efl*
economy	*eco*	ef·forts	*efls*
edit	*edl*	egg	*eq*
ed·ited	*edl-*	eggs	*egs*
edi·tion	*edy*	ei·ther	*elr*
edi·tions	*edys*	elder	*eldr*
edi·tor	*edlr*	elect	*elc*
edi·to·rial	*edlrel*	elected	*elc-*
edi·tors	*edlrs*	elec·tion	*elcy*
edu·cate	*eyca*	elec·tric	*elc*
edu·ca·tion	*eycy*	elec·tri·cal	*elcl*
edu·ca·tional	*eycyl*	elec·tri·cian	*ely*
edu·ca·tor	*eycar*	elec·tric·ity	*els'*
edu·ca·tors	*eycars*	elec·tron	*eln*
ef·fect	*efc*	elec·tronic	*elnc*
ef·fected	*efc-*	elec·tron·ics	*elncs*

Word	Shorthand	Word	Shorthand
ele·ment	*elm*	em·pha·size	*fsz*
ele·men·tary	*elmre*	em·ploy	*p*
ele·ments	*elms*	em·ployed	*p-*
ele·va·tion	*elv*	em·ployee	*pe*
ele·va·tor	*elvar*	em·ploy·ees	*pes*
ele·va·tors	*elvars*	em·ployer	*pr*
eli·gi·bil·ity	*eljßl*	em·ploy·ers	*prs*
eli·gi·ble	*eljß*	em·ploy·ing	*p_*
elimi·nate	*elma*	em·ploy·ment	*pm*
elimi·nated	*elma-*	em·ploys	*ps*
elimi·nates	*elmas*	empty	*e*
elimi·nat·ing	*elma_*	en·able	*nß*
elimi·na·tion	*elmy*	en·abled	*nß-*
else	*els*	en·ables	*nßs*
else·where	*els r*	en·abling	*nß_*
em·bank·ment	*bqm*	enact	*nac*
em·bar·rass·ment	*brsm*	en·acted	*nac-*
em·bassy	*bse*	enamel	*en l*
em·blem	*bl*	en·close	*enc*
emer·gen·cies	*e rjNes*	en·closed	*enc-*
emer·gency	*e rjNe*	en·closes	*encs*
emo·tional	*e jl*	en·clos·ing	*enc_*
em·pha·sis	*fss*	en·clo·sure	*enc*

en·clo·sures	*encs*	en·forced	*nfs-*
en·code	*ncd*	en·force·ment	*nfsm*
en·cod·ing	*ncd*	en·forces	*nfss*
en·com·pass·ing	*nkps*	en·forc·ing	*nfs*
en·coun·ter	*nkr*	en·gage	*ngj*
en·coun·tered	*nkr-*	en·gaged	*ngj-*
en·cour·age	*ncrj*	en·gage·ment	*ngjm*
en·cour·aged	*ncrj-*	en·gine	*njn*
en·cour·age·ment	*ncrjm*	en·gi·neer	*njnr*
en·cour·ag·ing	*ncrj*	en·gi·neer·ing	*njnr*
en·cy·clo·pe·dia	*nsclpda*	en·gi·neers	*njnrs*
end	*n*	en·gines	*njns*
en·deavor	*ndvr*	enjoy	*njy*
en·deav·or·ing	*ndvr*	en·joy·able	*njyß*
ended	*n-*	en·joyed	*njy-*
end·ing	*n*	en·joy·ing	*njy*
en·dorse	*ndrs*	en·joy·ment	*njym*
en·dorsed	*ndrs-*	en·joys	*njys*
en·dorse·ment	*ndrsm*	en·larged	*nlrj-*
en·dorse·ments	*ndrsms*	enough	*enf*
en·dow·ment	*ndom*	en·roll	*nrl*
en·ergy	*nrje*	en·rolled	*nrl-*
en·force	*nfs*	en·roll·ment	*nrlm*

Word	Shorthand	Word	Shorthand
en·tail	*ntl*	equal·iza·tion	*eqlz*
enter	*n*	equally	*eqll*
en·tered	*n-*	equals	*eqls*
en·ter·ing	*n̄*	equip	*eqp*
en·ter·prise	*nprz*	equip·ment	*eqpm*
en·ter·tain	*ntn*	equipped	*eqp-*
en·ter·tained	*ntn-*	eq·ui·ta·ble	*eqlB*
en·ter·tainer	*ntnr*	eq·uity	*eqle*
en·ter·tain·ing	*ntn̄*	equiva·lent	*eqvlN*
en·ter·tain·ment	*ntnm*	era	*era*
en·thu·si·asm	*ntzez*	erect	*erc*
en·thu·si·as·tic	*ntzesc*	error	*err*
en·thu·si·as·ti·cally	*ntzescl*	er·rors	*errs*
en·tire	*ntr*	es·crow	*escro*
en·tirely	*ntrl*	es·pe·cially	*esp*
en·ti·tled	*ntll-*	es·sence	*esN*
en·trance	*NrN*	es·sen·tial	*esnsl*
en·tries	*Nres*	es·sen·tially	*esnsll*
entry	*Nre*	es·tab·lish	*esl*
en·ve·lope	*env*	es·tab·lished	*esl-*
en·ve·lopes	*envs*	es·tab·lishes	*esls*
en·vi·ron·ment	*nvrnm*	es·tab·lish·ing	*esl̲*
equal	*eql*	es·tab·lish·ment	*eslm*

es·tab·lish·ments	*estms*	every	*E*
es·tate	*eSa*	eve·ry·body	*Ebde*
es·ti·mate	*eSa eSl* (v. / N.)	eve·ry·day	*Ed*
es·ti·mated	*eSa-*	eve·ry·one	*E1*
es·ti·mates	*eSas eSls* (v. / N.)	eve·ry·thing	*E*
es·ti·mat·ing	*eSa*	eve·ry·where	*Er*
et cet·era	*etc*	evi·dence	*evdN*
eth·ics	*etcs*	evi·denced	*evdN-*
evalu·ate	*evla*	evi·dent	*evdN*
evalu·ated	*evla-*	evi·dently	*evdNl*
evalu·at·ing	*evla*	exact	*vc*
evalu·ation	*evluy*	ex·actly	*vcl*
even	*evn*	exam	*v*
eve·ning	*evn*	ex·ami·na·tion	*vmy*
evenly	*evnl*	ex·ami·na·tions	*vmys*
event	*evN*	ex·am·ine	*vm*
events	*evNs*	ex·am·ined	*vm-*
even·tu·ally	*evnCull*	ex·am·iner	*vmr*
ever	*E*	ex·am·in·ers	*vmrs*
ev·er·green	*Egrn*	ex·am·in·ing	*vm*
ev·er·last·ing	*ElS*	ex·am·ple	*ex*
ev·er·last·ingly	*ElSl*	ex·am·ples	*exs*
ev·er·more	*E*	exams	*vs*

ex·ceed		ex·cuse	
ex·ceeded		exe·cute	
ex·ceed·ing		exe·cuted	
ex·ceed·ingly		exe·cu·tion	
ex·ceeds		ex·ecu·tive	
ex·cel·lent		ex·ecu·tives	
ex·cept		ex·empt	
ex·cepted		ex·emp·tion	
ex·cep·tion		ex·emp·tions	
ex·cep·tional		ex·er·cise	
ex·cep·tion·ally		ex·er·cises	
ex·cep·tions		ex·haust	
ex·cess		ex·hibit	
ex·ces·sive		ex·hib·its	
ex·change		exist	
ex·cise		ex·isted	
ex·cite		ex·is·tence	
ex·cite·ment		ex·ist·ing	
ex·cit·ing		ex·ists	
ex·cluded		ex·pand	
ex·clud·ing		ex·panded	
ex·clu·sive		ex·pand·ing	
ex·clu·sively		ex·pan·sion	

Word	Shorthand	Word	Shorthand
ex·pect	*(pc)*	ex·plained	*(pln-)*
ex·pected	*(pc-)*	ex·plain·ing	*(pln̲)*
ex·pect·ing	*(pc̲)*	ex·plains	*(plns)*
ex·pects	*(pcs)*	ex·pla·na·tion	*(plnj)*
ex·pe·dite	*(pdi)*	ex·pla·na·tions	*(plnjs)*
ex·pen·di·tures	*(pNCrs)*	ex·plo·ra·tion	*(plrj)*
ex·pense	*(pN)*	ex·plora·tory	*(plrtre)*
ex·penses	*(pNs)*	ex·plore	*(plr)*
ex·pen·sive	*(pNv)*	ex·plored	*(plr-)*
ex·pe·ri·ence	*(p)*	ex·plo·sion	*(plj)*
ex·pe·ri·enced	*(p-)*	ex·port	*(pt)*
ex·pe·ri·ences	*(ps)*	ex·ported	*(pt-)*
ex·pe·ri·enc·ing	*(p̲)*	ex·port·ing	*(pt̲)*
ex·peri·ment	*(prm)*	ex·ports	*(pts)*
ex·peri·men·tal	*(prml)*	ex·pose	*(pz)*
ex·peri·ments	*(prms)*	ex·posed	*(pz-)*
ex·pert	*(prt)*	ex·po·sure	*(pzr)*
ex·perts	*(prts)*	ex·po·sures	*(pzrs)*
ex·pi·ra·tion	*(prj)*	ex·press	*(prs)*
ex·pire	*(pr)*	ex·pressed	*(prs-)*
ex·pired	*(pr-)*	ex·press·ing	*(prs̲)*
ex·pires	*(prs)*	ex·pres·sion	*(prj)*
ex·plain	*(pln)*	ex·tend	*(N)*

Word	Outline	Word	Outline
ex·tended		faces	
ex·tend·ing		fac·ets	
ex·ten·sion		fa·cili·tate	
ex·ten·sive		fa·cil·ities	
ex·ten·sively		fa·cil·ity	
ex·tent		fac·ing	
ex·te·rior		fact	
ex·ter·nal		fac·tor	
extra		fac·to·ries	
ex·traor·di·nary		fac·tors	
ex·tra·sen·sory		fac·tory	
ex·treme		facts	
ex·tremely		fac·tual	
ex·tru·sion		fac·ulty	
eye		Fahrenheit	
		fail	
F		failed	
		fail·ure	
		fair	
fab·ric		fairly	
fab·ri·ca·tion		fair·ness	
fab·rics		faith	
face		faith·fully	
faced			

Word	Outline	Word	Outline
fall	* fl*	fault	*flt*
falls	*fls*	favor	*fvr*
fa·mil·iar	*fmlr*	fa·vor·able	*fvrß*
fa·mil·iar·ize	*fmlrz*	fa·vor·ably	*fvrß*
fami·lies	*fmls*	fa·vored	*fvr-*
family	*fml*	fa·vor·ite	*fvrl*
fa·mous	*fms*	fear	*fr*
fan	*fn*	fea·si·bil·ity	*fzßl*
fancy	*fnce*	fea·si·ble	*fzß*
far	*fr*	fea·ture	*fCr*
fare	*fr*	fea·tures	*fCrs*
fares	*frs*	fed·eral	*fed*
farm	*frm*	fed·er·al·ist	*fedS*
farmer	*frmr*	fed·er·al·ize	*fedz*
farm·ers	*frmrs*	fed·er·ally	*fedl*
farms	*frms*	fed·era·tion	*fdry*
fas·ci·nat·ing	*fsna*	fee	*fe*
fash·ion	*fj*	feed	*fd*
fash·ions	*fjs*	feed·ing	*fd*
fast	*fS*	feel	*fl*
faster	*fSr*	feel·ing	*fl*
fat	*fl*	feel·ings	*fl*
fa·ther	*flr*	feels	*fls*

fees	*fes*	files	*fls*
feet	*fl*	fil·ing	*fl-*
fell	*fl*	fill	*fl*
fel·low	*flo*	filled	*fl-*
fel·low·ship	*flos*	fill·ing	*fl-*
felt	*fll*	fills	*fls*
fe·male	*fml*	film	*flm*
fence	*fn*	films	*flms*
fer·til·izer	*frllzr*	fil·ters	*fllrs*
fes·ti·val	*fSvl*	final	*fnl*
few	*fu*	fi·nally	*fnll*
fewer	*fur*	fi·nance	*fnn*
fiber	*flr*	fi·nanced	*fnn-*
fic·tion	*fcy*	fi·nan·cial	*fnnsl*
fi·del·ity	*fdl*	fi·nanc·ing	*fnn-*
field	*fld*	find	*fn*
fields	*flds*	find·ing	*fn-*
fig·ure	*fgr*	find·ings	*fn=*
fig·ured	*fgr-*	finds	*fns*
fig·ures	*fgrs*	fine	*fn*
fig·ur·ing	*fgr-*	finer	*fnr*
file	*fl*	fin·est	*fns*
filed	*fl-*	fin·ish	*fns*

Word	Shorthand	Word	Shorthand
fin·ished	*fns-*	flags	*flgs*
fin·ish·ing	*fns_*	flame	*fl*
fire	*fr*	flam·ma·ble	*flB*
fires	*frs*	flat	*fll*
fir·ing	*fr_*	flat·tered	*fllr-*
firm	*fr*	fla·vor	*flvr*
firmer	*frr*	fla·vors	*flvrs*
firm·est	*frS*	fleet	*fle*
firmly	*frl*	flex·ibil·ity	*flxBl*
firm·ness	*fr'*	flight	*fle*
firms	*frs*	flights	*fles*
first	*frS 1S*	flood	*fld*
fis·cal	*fscl*	floor	*flr*
fish	*fs*	floors	*flrs*
fish·er·ies	*fsres*	flour	*flor*
fish·er·men	*fsrm*	flow	*flo*
fish·ery	*fsre*	flows	*flos*
fish·ing	*fs_*	fluid	*flud*
fit	*fl*	fly	*flu*
fits	*fls*	fly·ing	*flu_*
fixed	*fx-*	focus	*fcs*
fix·ture	*fxCr*	folder	*fldr*
fix·tures	*fxCrs*	fold·ers	*fldrs*

fold·ing	*fld*	fore·close	*fclz*
folks	*fcs*	forego	*fg*
fol·low	*flo*	fore·go·ing	*fg-*
fol·lowed	*flo-*	for·eign	*fm*
fol·low·ing	*flo*	fore·man	*fm*
fol·lows	*flos*	fore·men	*fm*
food	*fd*	fore·most	*fS*
foods	*fds*	fore·sight	*fsi*
foot	*ft*	for·est	*fS*
foot·age	*fy*	for·estry	*fSre*
foot·ball	*ftbl*	for·ests	*fSs*
foot·wear	*ftr*	for·ever	*fE*
for	*f*	forge	*ff*
for·bid	*fbd*	for·get	*fgt*
for·bid·den	*fbdn*	for·get·ful	*fgtf*
for·bid·ding	*fbd*	for·get·ting	*fgt*
for·bids	*fbds*	forg·ing	*ff-*
force	*fs*	for·give	*fgv*
forced	*fs-*	for·given	*fgvn*
forces	*fss*	for·give·ness	*fgv'*
forc·ing	*fs*	for·giv·ing	*fgv*
fore·cast	*fcS*	for·got	*fgt*
fore·casts	*fcSs*	for·got·ten	*fgtn*

Word	Shorthand	Word	Shorthand
fork·lift	*fclfl*	for·warded	*fw-*
form	*f*	for·ward·ing	*fw_*
for·mal	*fl*	found	*fon*
for·mally	*fll*	foun·da·tion	*fony*
for·mat	*fl*	founded	*fon-*
for·ma·tion	*fy*	frac·tion	*frcy*
formed	*fr-*	frame	*fr*
former	*frr*	frame·work	*frro*
for·merly	*frrl*	fram·ing	*fr_*
form·ing	*fr_*	fran·chise	*frncz*
forms	*frs*	fran·chises	*frnczs*
for·mula	*frla*	frank	*frq*
for·mu·late	*frla*	frankly	*frql*
for·mu·lated	*frla-*	free	*fre*
for·mu·la·tion	*frly*	free·dom	*fred*
fort	*fl*	freely	*frel*
forth	*fl*	freeze	*frz*
forth·com·ing	*flk_*	freight	*fra*
for·tu·nate	*fcnl*	fre·quency	*frqne*
for·tu·nately	*fcnll*	fre·quent	*frqn*
for·tune	*fcn*	fre·quently	*frqnl*
forum	*fr*	fresh	*frs*
for·ward	*fw*	friend	*frn*

friendly		fun·da·men·tal	
friends		fun·da·men·tals	
friend·ship		funded	
fringe		fund·ing	
from		funds	
front		funny	
frost·ing		fur·nace	
frosty		fur·nish	
fro·zen		fur·nished	
fuel		fur·nishes	
ful·fill		fur·nish·ing	
ful·filled		fur·nish·ings	
ful·fill·ing		fur·ni·ture	
ful·fill·ment		fur·ther	
full		fur·ther·more	
fuller		fuse	
full·est		fus·ing	
full·ness		fu·ture	
fully			
fun			
func·tion			
func·tions		gain	
fund		gained	

G

Word	Outline	Word	Outline
gains	*gns*	gen·er·al·ized	*jnz-*
gal·ley	*gle*	gen·er·al·izes	*jnzs*
gal·lon	*gln*	gen·er·al·iz·ing	*jnz-*
gal·lons	*glns*	gen·er·al·ly	*jnl*
gal·va·nized	*glvnz-*	gen·er·ated	*jnra-*
game	*g*	gen·er·ous	*jnrs*
games	*gs*	ge·net·ics	*jnlcs*
gap	*gp*	gen·tle·man	*jNlm*
ga·rage	*grj*	gen·tle·men	*jNlm*
gas	*gs*	genu·ine	*jnun*
gaso·line	*gsln*	get	*gl*
gate	*ga*	gets	*gls*
gath·er·ing	*glr-*	get·ting	*gl-*
gauge	*gj*	giant	*juN*
gave	*gv*	gift	*gfl*
gear	*gr*	gifts	*gfls*
geared	*gr-*	girl	*grl*
gen·eral	*jn*	girl·hood	*grlh*
gen·er·al·ist	*jnS*	girls	*grls*
gen·er·al·ity	*jnl*	give	*gv*
gen·er·al·iza·tion	*jnzj*	given	*gvn*
gen·er·al·iza·tions	*jnzjs*	gives	*gvs*
gen·er·al·ize	*jnz*	giv·ing	*gv-*

Word	Outline	Word	Outline
glad	*gld*	gov·ern·ing	*gvrn̲*
gladly	*gldl*	gov·ern·ment	*gvt*
glands	*glNs*	gov·ern·mental	*gvtl*
glass	*gls*	gov·ern·ments	*gvts*
globe	*glb*	gov·er·nor	*gvrnr*
gloss	*gls*	gov·er·nors	*gvrnrs*
glossy	*glse*	grade	*grd*
go	*g*	grades	*grds*
goal	*gl*	gradu·ate	v. *grja* adj. or N. *grjul*
goals	*gls*	gradu·ated	*grja-*
goes	*gs*	gradu·ates	v. *grjas* N. *grjuls*
going	*g̲*	gradu·at·ing	*grja̲*
gold	*gld*	gradu·ation	*grjuy*
golden	*gldn*	grain	*grn*
golf	*glf*	grand	*grN*
gone	*gn*	grant	*grN*
good	*g.*	granted	*grN-*
goodly	*gl*	grant·ing	*grN̲*
good·ness	*g'*	grants	*grNs*
goods	*gs*	graph·ite	*grfi*
good·will	*gl*	grass	*grs*
got	*gl*	grate	*gr*
gov·ern	*gvrn*	grate·ful	*grf*

grate·fully	*grfl*	grow·ing	*gro_*
grati·fy·ing	*grlf_*	grown	*grn*
grati·tude	*grlld*	growth	*grl*
gray	*gra*	guar·an·tee	*grnte*
graz·ing	*grz_*	guar·an·teed	*grnte-*
great	*gr*	guar·an·tee·ing	*grnte_*
greater	*grr*	guar·an·tees	*grntes*
great·est	*grs*	guard	*grd*
greatly	*grl*	guardian	*grden*
great·ness	*gr'*	guess	*gs*
green	*grn*	guest	*gs*
greet·ings	*gre_*	guests	*gss*
gro·cery	*grsre*	gui·dance	*gdN*
gross	*grs*	guide	*gd*
ground	*groN*	guided	*gd-*
grounds	*groNs*	guide·lines	*gdlns*
group	*grp*	gulf	*glf*
groups	*grps*	gun	*gn*
grove	*grv*	gym·na·sium	*jmze*
groves	*grvs*	gyp·sum	*jps*
grow	*gro*		
grower	*gror*		
grow·ers	*grors*		

H

habit	*hbl*	hap·pen	*hpn*
habi·tat	*hbll*	hap·pened	*hpn-*
hab·its	*hbls*	hap·pen·ing	*hpn̲*
had	*h*	hap·pens	*hpns*
hadn't	*hN*	hap·pi·ness	*hpe'*
hair	*hr*	happy	*hpe*
half	*hf*	hard	*hrd*
hall	*hl*	hard·ship	*hrds*
ham·mer	*h⌒r*	hard·ware	*hrd⌒*
ham·mers	*h⌒rs*	har·vest	*hrvs*
hand	*hN*	has	*hs*
hand·book	*hNbc*	hasn't	*hsN*
handi·cap	*hNcp*	hate	*ha*
handi·capped	*hNcp-*	have	*v*
han·dle	*hNl*	haven't	*vN*
han·dled	*hNl-*	hav·ing	*v̲*
han·dles	*hNls*	haz·ard	*hzrd*
han·dling	*hNl̄*	haz·ards	*hzrds*
hands	*hNs̄*	he	*h*
hand·some	*hN⌒*	he's	*h's*
handy	*hNe*	head	*hd*
		head·ache	*hdac*
		headed	*hd-*

head·ing	*hd*	help	*hlp*
head·quar·ters	*hdqlrs*	helped	*hlp-*
heads	*hds*	help·ful	*hlpf*
health	*hlt*	help·ing	*hlp*
healthy	*hlte*	helps	*hlps*
hear	*hr*	hemi·sphere	*h∼sfr*
heard	*hrd*	hence	*hM*
hear·ing	*hr*	her	*hr*
hear·ings	*hr*	herb	*erb*
heart	*hrt*	here	*hr*
hearty	*hrte*	here's	*hrs*
heat	*he*	here·af·ter	*hraf*
heater	*her*	hereby	*hrb*
heat·ing	*he*	herein	*hrn*
heavier	*hver*	hereof	*hrv*
heavily	*hvl*	hereto	*hrt*
heavy	*hve*	here·to·fore	*hrtf*
hedge	*hy*	here·un·der	*hru*
heeded	*hd-*	here·with	*hr*
height	*hi*	heri·tage	*hrt*
heirs	*ars*	hers	*hrs*
held	*hld*	her·self	*hrsf*
hello	*hlo*	hesi·tate	*hzta*

high	*hi*	hold·ing	*hld*
higher	*hir*	hold·ings	*hld*
high·est	*his*	holds	*hlds*
high·lights	*hilis*	hole	*hl*
highly	*hil*	holes	*hls*
high·way	*hi a*	holi·day	*hld*
hill	*hl*	holi·days	*hlds*
hills	*hls*	home	*h*
him	*h*	home·own·ers	*h ors*
him·self	*hsf*	homes	*h s*
hire	*hr*	honor	*onr*
hired	*hr-*	hon·or·able	*onrß*
hir·ing	*hr*	hon·ored	*onr-*
his	*)*	hook	*hc*
his·to·ri·ans	*hSrens*	hoot	*hu*
his·tor·ical	*hSrcl*	hope	*hp*
his·to·ries	*hSres*	hoped	*hp-*
his·tory	*hSre*	hope·ful	*hpf*
hit	*ht*	hope·fully	*hpfl*
hobby	*hbe*	hope·less	*hpls*
hold	*hld*	hope·lessly	*hplsl*
holder	*hldr*	hopes	*hps*
hold·ers	*hldrs*	hop·ing	*hp*

ho·ri·zon	*hrzn*	hous·ing	*hoz-*
ho·ri·zons	*hrzns*	how	*ho*
hose	*hz*	how·ever	*hoE*
hos·pi·tal	*hsp*	human	*hm*
hos·pi·tal·ity	*hspll*	hum·ble	*h B*
hos·pi·tal·iza·tion	*hspzj*	hun·dred	*H*
hos·pi·tal·ize	*hspz*	hun·dreds	*Hs*
hos·pi·tal·ized	*hspz-*	hun·dredth	*HL*
hos·pi·tal·izes	*hspzs*	hurry	*hre*
hos·pi·tal·iz·ing	*hspz-*	hurt	*hrl*
hos·pi·tals	*hsps*	hus·band	*hzbN*
host	*hS*	hy·drant	*hdrN*
hot	*hl*	hy·drau·lic	*hdrlc*
hotel	*hll*	hy·dro·elec·tric	*hdrelc*
ho·tels	*hlls*	hy·giene	*hyn*
hour	*hr*		
hour·glass	*hrgls*		**I**
hourly	*hrl*		
hours	*hrs*	I	*ι*
house	*hŏs hŏz*	I'd	*ι'd*
house·hold	*hoshld*	I'll	*ι'l*
house·keep·ing	*hoscp-*	I'm	*ι'*
houses	*hoss*	I've	*ι'v*

ice		im·pact	
idea		im·part	
ideal		im·parted	
ideas		im·part·ing	
iden·ti·cal		im·parts	
iden·ti·fi·ca·tion		im·pa·tient	
iden·ti·fied		im·pera·tive	
iden·tify		im·ple·ment	
iden·ti·fy·ing		im·ple·men·ta·tion	
if		im·ple·mented	
ill		im·ple·ment·ing	
ill·ness		im·port	
il·lus·trate		im·por·tance	
il·lus·trated		im·por·tant	
il·lus·trat·ing		im·por·tantly	
il·lus·tra·tion		im·ported	
il·lus·tra·tions		im·port·ing	
image		im·ports	
im·agi·na·tion		im·pose	
im·ag·ine		im·posed	
im·me·di·ate		im·po·si·tion	
im·me·di·ately		im·pos·si·ble	
im·me·di·ate·ness		im·press	

im·pressed		in·clem·ent	
im·pres·sion		in·clined	
im·pres·sive		in·clude	
im·printed		in·cluded	
im·proper		in·cludes	
im·prove		in·clud·ing	
im·proved		in·clu·sion	
im·prove·ment		in·clu·sive	
im·prove·ments		in·come	
im·proves		in·com·plete	
im·prov·ing		in·con·ven·ience	
in		in·con·ven·ienced	
in·abil·ity		in·con·ven·iences	
in·ad·ver·tently		in·con·ven·ienc·ing	
in·as·much		in·con·ven·ient	
in·cep·tion		in·cor·po·rate	
inch		in·cor·po·rated	
inched		in·cor·po·rates	
inches		in·cor·po·rat·ing	
inch·ing		in·cor·po·ra·tion	
in·ci·dent		in·cor·po·ra·tions	
in·ci·den·tal		in·cor·rect	
in·ci·den·tally		in·crease	

Word	Outline	Word	Outline
in·creased	*ncrs–*	in·di·rect	*ndr*
in·creases	*ncrss*	in·di·rectly	*ndrl*
in·creas·ing	*ncrs̲*	in·di·vidual	*Nv*
in·creas·ingly	*ncrsf*	in·di·vidu·al·ist	*NvS*
in·cre·ments	*ncrms*	in·di·vidu·al·ity	*Nvᶫ*
in·cu·ba·tor	*ncbar*	in·di·vidu·ally	*Nvl*
in·cu·ba·tors	*ncbars*	in·di·vidu·als	*Nvs*
in·curred	*ncr–*	in·dulge	*ndlj*
in·debted	*ndt–*	in·dus·trial	*Nl*
in·debt·ed·ness	*ndt–'*	in·dus·tri·al·ism	*Nlz*
in·deed	*ndd*	in·dus·tri·al·ist	*NlS*
in·dem·nity	*nd nle*	in·dus·tri·al·iza·tion	*Nlzj*
in·de·pend·ence	*NpNN*	in·dus·tri·al·ize	*Nlz*
in·de·pend·ent	*NpNN*	in·dus·tri·al·izes	*Nlzs*
index	*Nx*	in·dus·tri·ally	*Nll*
in·di·cate	*Nca*	in·dus·tries	*Ns*
in·di·cated	*Nca–*	in·dus·tri·ous	*Ns*
in·di·cates	*Ncas*	in·dus·tri·ously	*Nsl*
in·di·cat·ing	*Nca̲*	in·dus·tri·ous·ness	*Ns'*
in·di·ca·tion	*Ncj*	in·dus·try	*N*
in·dif·fer·ent	*ndfrN*	in·evi·ta·ble	*nevlB*
in·di·gent	*NjN*	in·evi·ta·bly	*nevlB*
in·dig·nant	*ndgnN*	in·ex·pen·sive	*nxpNv*

Word	Shorthand	Word	Shorthand
in·ex·pe·ri·ence	*nxp*	in·jured	*njr-*
in·ex·pe·ri·enced	*nxp-*	in·ju·ries	*njres*
in·fir·mary	*nfrre*	in·jury	*njre*
in·fla·tion	*nfly*	ink	*iq*
in·fla·tion·ary	*nflyre*	inks	*iqs*
in·flu·ence	*nfluN*	in·land	*nlN*
in·flu·en·tial	*nflunsl*	in·mate	*n a*
in·form	*nf*	in·mates	*n as*
in·for·mal	*nfl*	inn	*n*
in·for·ma·tion	*inf*	inner	*nr*
in·for·ma·tional	*infl*	in·no·va·tion	*nvy*
in·forma·tive	*nfw*	in·op·era·tive	*nopv*
in·formed	*nf-*	input	*npl*
in·form·ing	*nf*	in·quire	*nq*
in·forms	*nfs*	in·quired	*nq-*
in·habi·tants	*nhblNs*	in·quir·ies	*nqes*
in·heri·tance	*nhrlN*	in·quir·ing	*nq-*
ini·tial	*insl*	in·quiry	*nqe*
ini·tially	*insll*	in·sert	*nsrl*
ini·ti·ate	*insa inšel*	in·serted	*nsrl-*
ini·ti·ated	*insa-*	in·ser·tion	*nsry*
ini·tia·tion	*nsey*	in·serts	*nsrls*
in·jec·tion	*njcy*	in·side	*nsd*

Word	Shorthand	Word	Shorthand
in·sight	*nsi*	in·struct	*nSrc*
in·sist	*nsS*	in·structed	*nSrc-*
in·so·far	*nsofr*	in·struc·tion	*nSrcy*
in·spect	*nspc*	in·struc·tional	*nSrcyl*
in·spected	*nspc-*	in·struc·tions	*nSrcys*
in·spec·tion	*nspcy*	in·struc·tor	*nSrcr*
in·spec·tors	*nspcrs*	in·struc·tors	*nSrcrs*
in·spi·ra·tion	*nspry*	in·stru·ment	*nSrm*
in·stall	*nSl*	in·stru·ments	*nSrms*
in·stal·la·tion	*nSly*	in·suf·fi·cient	*nsfsN*
in·stal·la·tions	*nSlys*	in·sur·abil·ity	*nsrßL*
in·stalled	*nSl-*	in·sur·able	*nsrß*
in·stall·ing	*nSl_*	in·sur·ance	*ins*
in·stall·ment	*nSlm*	in·sure	*nsr*
in·stall·ments	*nSlms*	in·sured	*nsr-*
in·stance	*nSN*	in·sur·ing	*nsr_*
in·stances	*nSNs*	in·teg·rity	*ntgrte*
in·stant	*nSN*	in·tel·lec·tual	*Nlccul*
in·stead	*nSd*	in·tel·li·gence	*nllyN*
in·sti·tute	*nSlu*	in·tel·li·gent	*nllyN*
in·sti·tu·tion	*nSly*	in·tend	*nlN*
in·sti·tu·tional	*nSlyl*	in·tended	*nlN-*
in·sti·tu·tions	*nSlys*	in·tense	*nlN*

in·ten·sive		into	
in·tent		in·toxi·cants	
in·ten·tion		in·tra·mu·ral	
in·ter·change		in·trigu·ing	
in·ter·est		in·tro·duce	
in·ter·ested		in·tro·duced	
in·ter·est·ing		in·tro·duc·ing	
in·ter·ests		in·tro·duc·tion	
in·ter·fere		in·tro·duc·tory	
in·terim		in·valu·able	
in·te·rior		in·ven·tion	
in·ter·me·di·ate		in·ven·to·ries	
in·ter·nal		in·ven·tory	
in·ter·na·tional		in·vest	
in·ter·pret		in·vested	
in·ter·pre·ta·tion		in·ves·ti·gate	
in·ter·state		in·ves·ti·gated	
in·ter·val		in·ves·ti·gat·ing	
in·ter·vals		in·ves·ti·ga·tion	
in·ter·ven·ing		in·ves·ti·ga·tions	
in·ter·view		in·vest·ment	
in·ter·view·ing		in·vest·ments	
in·ter·views		in·ves·tors	

in·vi·ta·tion		is·sues	
in·vite		is·su·ing	
in·vited		it	
in·vit·ing		it's	
in·voice		item	
in·voiced		item·ized	
in·voices		items	
in·voic·ing		its	
in·volve		it·self	
in·volved		ivory	
in·volve·ment			
in·volves			
in·volv·ing		**J**	
iron		jacket	
irons		jani·tor	
ir·regu·lar		jet	
ir·ri·ga·tion		jew·elry	
is		jew·els	
is·land		job	
isn't		job·ber	
is·su·ance		jobs	
issue		join	
is·sued		joined	

join·ing	*jyn_*			
joins	*jyns*			
joint	*jyN*	keen	*cn*	
jointly	*jyNl*	keep	*cp*	
jour·nal	*jrnl*	keep·ing	*cp_*	
judge	*jj*	keeps	*cps*	
judges	*jjs*	kept	*cpt*	
judg·ment	*jjm*	key	*ce*	
judg·ments	*jjms*	key·board	*cebrd*	
ju·di·ci·ary	*jdsere*	key punch	*ce pnC*	
jun·ior	*jr*	keys	*ces*	
jun·iors	*jrs*	kill	*cl*	
jur·is·dic·tion	*jrsdcy*	killed	*cl-*	
jury	*jre*	kind	*cN*	
just	*jS*	kind·est	*cNS*	
jus·tice	*jSs*	kindly	*cNl*	
jus·ti·fi·ca·tion	*jSfy*	kinds	*cNs*	
jus·ti·fied	*jSf-*	kit	*ct*	
jus·tify	*jSf*	kitchen	*cCn*	
ju·ve·nile	*jvnl*	kits	*cts*	
		knew	*nu*	
		know	*no*	
		know·ing	*no_*	

K

knowl·edge	*nly*	land·own·ers	*lNors*
known	*nn*	lands	*lNs*
knows	*nos*	lane	*ln*
		lanes	*lns*
		lan·guage	*lgy*
L		lapse	*lps*
		lapsed	*lps-*
label	*lB*	large	*ly*
la·beled	*lB-*	largely	*lyl*
la·bel·ing	*lB̲*	larger	*lyr*
la·bels	*lBs*	larg·est	*lyS*
labor	*lbr*	last	*lS*
labo·ra·to·ries	*lbrtres*	late	*la*
labo·ra·tory	*lbrtre*	later	*lar*
la·bor·ers	*lbrrs*	lat·est	*laS*
lack	*lc*	lat·ter	*llr*
la·dies	*ldes*	launch	*lnC*
lad·ing	*ld̲*	launch·ing	*lnC̲*
lady	*lde*	launch·ings	*lnC̲̲*
lake	*lc*	law	*la*
lakes	*lcs*	lawn	*ln*
lamp	*lp*	laws	*las*
lamps	*lps*	law·yer	*lar*
land	*lN*		

word	shorthand	word	shorthand
law·yers	*lars*	leaves	*lvs*
lay	*la*	leav·ing	*lv*
lay·out	*laot*	lec·ture	*lcCr*
lead	*ld*	led	*ld*
leader	*ldr*	ledger	*ljr*
lead·ers	*ldrs*	left	*lft*
lead·er·ship	*ldrs*	legal	*lgl*
lead·ing	*ld*	leg·is·la·tion	*ljslj*
leads	*lds*	leg·is·la·tive	*ljslv*
leaf	*lf*	leg·is·la·ture	*ljslCr*
leaf·let	*lflt*	lend	*ln*
league	*lg*	lend·ing	*ln*
lean·ing	*ln*	length	*lgt*
learn	*lrn*	lengths	*lgts*
learned	*lrn-*	lens	*lnz*
learn·ing	*lrn*	less	*ls*
lease	*ls*	les·son	*lsn*
leased	*ls-*	let	*ll*
leases	*lss*	let's	*ll's*
leas·ing	*ls*	lets	*lls*
least	*lS*	let·ter	*L*
leather	*llr*	let·ter·head	*Lhd*
leave	*lv*	let·ter·ing	*L*

let·ters	*Ls*	light	*li*
let·ting	*ll*	light·ing	*li*
level	*lvl*	lights	*lis*
lev·els	*lvls*	like	*lc*
li·abil·ities	*liB^ls*	like·li·hood	*lclh*
li·abil·ity	*liB^l*	likely	*lcl*
li·able	*liB*	like·wise	*lcz*
li·ai·son	*lezn*	lime	*l*
lib·eral	*lbrl*	limit	*lit*
lib·erty	*lbrle*	limi·ta·tion	*lty*
li·brary	*lbrre*	limi·ta·tions	*ltys*
li·cense	*lsN*	lim·ited	*lit-*
li·censed	*lsN-*	lim·its	*lits*
li·censes	*lsNs*	line	*ln*
li·cens·ing	*lsN*	lineal	*lnel*
lie	*li*	linear	*lner*
lien	*ln*	lined	*ln-*
lies	*lis*	lin·ens	*lnns*
lieu	*lu*	lines	*lns*
life	*lf*	liq·uid	*lqd*
life·time	*lft*	liq·ui·date	*lqda*
lift	*lft*	list	*lS*
lifts	*lfts*	listed	*lS-*

lis·ten	*lsn*	lo·cal·ity	*lcl*
lis·tened	*lsn-*	lo·cally	*lcll*
lis·ten·ing	*lsn*	lo·cate	*lca*
list·ing	*lš*	lo·cated	*lca-*
list·ings	*lš*	lo·ca·tion	*lcy*
lists	*lšs*	lo·ca·tions	*lcys*
lit·er·ally	*llrll*	lock·ers	*lcrs*
lit·era·ture	*lel*	locks	*lcs*
lit·tle	*lll*	lodge	*ly*
live	*lv*	lodges	*lys*
lived	*lv-*	log	*lq*
lively	*lvl*	log·ical	*lycl*
lives	*lvs*	long	*lg*
live·stock	*lvSc*	longer	*lgr*
liv·ing	*lv*	long·est	*lgs*
load	*ld*	look	*lc*
loaded	*ld-*	looked	*lc-*
load·ing	*ld*	look·ing	*lc*
loads	*lds*	looks	*lcs*
loan	*ln*	loop	*lp*
loans	*lns*	loose	*ls*
lobby	*lbe*	lose	*lz*
local	*lcl*	loss	*ls*

losses	*lss*		**M**	
lost	*lS*			
lot	*ll*	ma·chine	*An*	
lots	*lls*	ma·chin·ery	*Anre*	
lounge	*lony*	ma·chines	*Ans*	
love	*lv*	mad	*d*	
loved	*lv-*	made	*d*	
low	*lo*	maga·zine	*gzn*	
lower	*lor*	maga·zines	*gzns*	
low·ered	*lor-*	magic	*yc*	
low·est	*loS*	mag·nifi·cent	*gnfsN*	
loyal	*lyl*	mail	*l*	
loy·alty	*lylle*	mailed	*l-*	
lu·bri·ca·tion	*lbrcy*	mailer	*lr*	
luck	*lc*	mail·ing	*l*	
lucky	*lce*	mail·ings	*l*	
lug·gage	*lgj*	main	*m*	
lump	*l p*	mainly	*ml*	
lunch	*lnC*	mains	*ms*	
lunch·eon	*lnCn*	main·tain	*mln*	
		main·tained	*mln-*	
		main·tain·ing	*mln*	
		main·tains	*mlns*	

main·te·nance	*ntnN*	manned	*n-*
major	*jr*	man·ner	*nr*
ma·jor·ity	*jrt*	man·power	*npor*
ma·jors	*jrs*	manual	*nul*
make	*c*	manu·als	*nuls*
maker	*cr*	manu·fac·ture	*f*
mak·ers	*crs*	manu·fac·tured	*f-*
makes	*cs*	manu·fac·turer	*fr*
mak·ing	*c*	manu·fac·tur·ers	*frs*
male	*l*	manu·fac·tures	*fs*
ma·li·cious	*lss*	manu·fac·tur·ing	*f-*
man	*n*	many	*me*
man·age	*j*	map	*p*
man·aged	*j-*	maps	*ps*
man·age·ment	*jm*	mar·ginal	*rjnl*
man·age·ments	*jms*	ma·rine	*rn*
man·ager	*jr*	mark	*rc*
mana·gerial	*jrel*	marked	*rc-*
man·ag·ers	*jrs*	mar·ket	*r*
man·ages	*js*	mar·keted	*r-*
man·ag·ing	*j-*	mar·ket·ing	*r*
man·da·tory	*Ntre*	mar·kets	*rs*
man-hours	*n = hrs*	mark·ing	*rc*

marks	*rcs*	maybe	*ab*
mar·riage	*ry*	mayor	*ar*
mar·ried	*re-*	me	*e*
marsh	*rs*	meal	*l*
mass	*s*	meals	*ls*
mas·ter	*Sr*	mean	*m*
mas·ters	*Srs*	mean·ing	*m_*
mat	*l*	mean·ing·ful	*mf*
match	*C*	means	*ms*
match·ing	*C_*	meant	*m*
ma·te·rial	*lrel*	mean·time	*ml*
ma·te·ri·als	*lrels*	mean·while	*ml*
mathe·mat·ical	*ldcl*	meas·ure	*zr*
mathe·mat·ics	*ldcs*	meas·ured	*zr-*
mats	*ls*	meas·ure·ment	*zrm*
mat·ter	*lr*	meas·ure·ments	*zrms*
mat·ters	*lrs*	meas·ures	*zrs*
mat·tress	*lrs*	meat	*e*
ma·ture	*lr*	me·chan·ical	*cncl*
ma·tured	*lr-*	me·chan·ics	*cncs*
ma·tur·ity	*lr^l*	mecha·nism	*cnz*
maxi·mum	*xm*	mecha·nized	*cnz-*
may	*a*	media	*da*

med·ical	_dcl_	mer·can·tile	_rcntl_
medi·care	_dcr_	mer·chan·dise	_dse_
medi·cine	_dsn_	mer·chan·dises	_dses_
me·dium	_de_	mer·chan·dis·ing	_dse_
meet	_e_	mer·chant	_rCN_
meet·ing	_e_	mer·cury	_rcre_
meet·ings	_e_	mere	_r_
meets	_es_	merely	_rl_
mel·low	_lo_	merger	_ryr_
mem·ber	_mbr_	merit	_rl_
mem·bers	_mbrs_	mer·its	_rls_
mem·ber·ship	_mbrs_	merry	_re_
mem·ber·ships	_mbrss_	mes·sage	_sy_
memo	_mo_	met	_t_
memo·ran·dum	_mrN_	metal	_tl_
me·mo·rial	_rel_	me·tal·lic	_tlc_
memory	_mre_	met·als	_tls_
memos	_mos_	meter	_m_
men	_m_	me·ters	_ms_
men·tal	_mll_	method	_td_
men·tion	_my_	meth·ods	_tds_
men·tioned	_my-_	met·ro·poli·tan	_trplln_
menu	_mu_	mid·dle	_dl_

Word	Outline	Word	Outline
might		min·utes	
mile		mir·rors	
mile·age		mis·cel·la·ne·ous	
miles		mis·lay	
mili·tary		mis·lead	
milk		mis·place	
mill		mis·placed	
mil·lion		mis·print	
mil·lion·aire		miss	
mil·lions		missed	
mil·lionth		miss·ing	
mills		mis·sion	
mind		mis·take	
minds		mis·taken	
mine		mis·un·der·stand	
min·eral		mis·un·der·stand·ing	
min·er·als		mis·un·der·stands	
mini·mize		mis·un·der·stood	
mini·mum		mix	
min·ing		mixed	
minor		mix·ing	
mi·nor·ity		mo·bile	
min·ute		mode	

model	_dl_	mother	_lr_
mod·els	_dls_	mo·tion	_q_
mod·ern	_drn_	motor	_lr_
mod·est	_ds_	mo·tors	_lrs_
modi·fi·ca·tion	_dfy_	mount	_oN_
modi·fi·ca·tions	_dfys_	moun·tain	_oNn_
modi·fied	_df-_	mounted	_oN-_
modify	_df_	move	_v_
mo·ment	_m_	moved	_v-_
money	_me_	move·ment	_vm_
month	_o_	move·ments	_vms_
monthly	_ol_	moves	_vs_
months	_os_	movie	_ve_
moral	_rl_	mov·ies	_ves_
more	_—_	mov·ing	_v_
more·over	_o_	Mr.	_r_
morn·ing	_rn_	Mrs.	_rs_
mort·gage	_rgy_	Ms.	_s_
mort·ga·gee	_rgje_	much	_c_
mort·gages	_rgjs_	mud	_d_
most	_s_	mul·ti·ple	_llpl_
motel	_ll_	mu·nici·pal	_nspl_
mo·tels	_lls_	mu·seum	_ze_

music	*zc*	na·tion·als	*nyls*
mu·si·cians	*zjs*	na·tions	*nys*
must	*S*	na·tion·wide	*nyd*
mus·ter	*Sr*	na·tive	*nv*
mu·tual	*Cul*	natu·ral	*nCrl*
mu·tu·ally	*Cull*	natu·rally	*nCrll*
my	*u*	na·ture	*nCr*
my·self	*usf*	navel	*nvl*
mys·te·ri·ous	*Mlres*	navy	*nve*
mys·tery	*Mlre*	near	*nr*
		nearby	*nrb*
		near·est	*nrS*
	N	nearly	*nrl*
		nec·es·sarily	*nesl*
name	*n*	nec·es·sary	*nes*
named	*n-*	ne·ces·si·tate	*nssta*
name·less	*nls*	ne·ces·sity	*nssᶜ*
namely	*nl*	need	*nd*
names	*ns*	needed	*nd-*
nar·rate	*nra*	need·less	*ndls*
nar·ra·tive	*nrv*	needs	*nds*
na·tion	*ny*	nega·tive	*ngv*
na·tional	*nyl*	ne·glected	*nglc-*
na·tion·ally	*nyll*		

Word	Shorthand	Word	Shorthand
ne·go·ti·ate	*ngsa*	no	*no*
ne·go·ti·ated	*ngsa-*	nomi·nal	*nml*
ne·go·ti·at·ing	*ngsa_*	nomi·nate	*nma*
ne·go·tia·tion	*ngsej*	nomi·nated	*nma-*
ne·go·tia·tions	*ngsejs*	nomi·na·tion	*nmy*
neigh·bor·hood	*nbrh*	nomi·na·tions	*nmys*
nei·ther	*ntr*	none	*nn*
net	*nt*	non·profit	*nnpft*
net·work	*nto*	noon	*nn*
neu·tral	*ntrl*	nor	*nr*
never	*nvr*	nor·mal	*nrl*
nev·er·the·less	*nvrls*	nor·mally	*nrll*
new	*nu*	north	*N*
newest	*nus*	north·east	*NE*
newly	*nul*	north·east·erly	*NErl*
news	*nz*	north·east·ern	*NErn*
news·let·ter	*nzL*	north·ern	*Nrn*
news·pa·per	*nzppr*	north·ward	*Nw*
news·pa·pers	*nzpprs*	north·west	*NW*
next	*nx*	north·west·ern	*NWrn*
nice	*ns*	nose	*nz*
night	*nu*	not	*n*
nights	*nus*	no·tary	*ntre*

no·ta·tion	*nly*	num·ber·less	*Nols*
no·ta·tions	*nlys*	num·bers	*Nos*
note	*nl*	nu·mer·ous	*n~rs*
noted	*nl-*	nurse	*nrs*
notes	*nls*	nurs·ery	*nrsre*
noth·ing	*nlg*	nurses	*nrss*
no·tice	*nls*	nurs·ing	*nrs_*
no·tice·able	*nlsB*	nut·shell	*nlsl*
no·tice·ably	*nlsB*		
no·ticed	*nls-*		
no·tices	*nlss*		
no·ti·fi·ca·tion	*nlff*	ob·ject	*obyc*
no·ti·fied	*nlf-*	ob·jec·tion	*obycy*
no·ti·fies	*nlfs*	ob·jec·tions	*obycys*
no·tify	*nlf*	ob·jec·tive	*obycv*
no·ti·fy·ing	*nlf_*	ob·jec·tives	*obycvs*
not·with·stand·ing	*n SN*	ob·li·gated	*oblga-*
now	*no*	ob·li·ga·tion	*oblgy*
noz·zle	*nzl*	ob·li·ga·tions	*oblgys*
nu·clear	*ncler*	oblige	*obly*
num·ber	*No*	ob·ser·vance	*obzrvN*
num·bered	*No-*	ob·ser·va·tion	*obzrvy*
num·ber·ing	*No_*	ob·ser·va·tions	*obzrvys*

O

ob·serve	*obzrv*	oc·curs	*ocrs*
ob·served	*obzrv-*	ocean	*oy*
ob·so·lete	*obsle*	odd	*od*
ob·tain	*obln*	of	*v*
ob·tain·able	*oblnB*	off	*of*
ob·tained	*obln-*	offer	*ofr*
ob·tain·ing	*obln*	of·fered	*ofr-*
ob·vi·ous	*obves*	of·fer·ing	*ofr*
ob·vi·ously	*obvesl*	of·fer·ings	*ofr*
oc·ca·sion	*ocy*	of·fers	*ofrs*
oc·ca·sional	*ocyl*	of·fice	*ofs*
oc·ca·sion·ally	*ocyll*	of·fi·cer	*ofsr*
oc·ca·sions	*ocys*	of·fi·cers	*ofsrs*
oc·cu·pancy	*ocpNe*	of·fices	*ofss*
oc·cu·pa·tion	*ocpy*	of·fi·cial	*ofsl*
oc·cu·pa·tional	*ocpyl*	of·fi·cially	*ofsll*
oc·cu·pa·tions	*ocpys*	of·fi·cials	*ofsls*
oc·cu·pied	*ocpi-*	off·set	*ofsl*
oc·cupy	*ocpi*	often	*ofn*
occur	*ocr*	oil	*yl*
oc·curred	*ocr-*	oils	*yls*
oc·cur·rence	*ocrN*	okay	*ok*
oc·cur·ring	*ocr*	old	*old*

Word	Outline	Word	Outline
older	*oldr*	op·er·at·ing	*op-*
omit		op·era·tion	
omit·ted		op·era·tional	
on		op·era·tion·ally	
once		op·era·tions	
on·com·ing		op·era·tor	
on·go·ing		op·era·tors	
on·looker		opin·ion	
on·look·ing		opin·ion·ated	
only		opin·ions	
on·rush		op·por·tu·ni·ties	
onset		op·por·tu·nity	
onto		op·posed	
on·ward		op·po·si·tion	
on·wards		op·ti·mum	
open		op·tion	
opened		op·tional	
open·ing		op·tions	
open·ings		or	
opens		oral	
op·er·ate		or·ange	
op·er·ated		orbit	
op·er·ates		order	

or·dered	*od-*	origi·nally	*orynll*
or·der·ing	*od*	origi·nals	*orynls*
or·der·lies	*odls*	origi·nate	*oryna*
or·der·li·ness	*odl'*	origi·nat·ing	*oryna*
or·derly	*odl*	or·tho·pe·dic	*orlpdc*
or·ders	*ods*	other	*ol*
or·di·nance	*ordnN*	oth·ers	*ols*
or·di·narily	*ordl*	oth·er·wise	*olz*
or·di·nary	*ord*	ought	*ol*
or·gan·iza·tion	*ogj*	ounce	*oz*
or·gan·iza·tional	*ogjl*	ounces	*ozs*
or·gan·iza·tion·ally	*ogjll*	our	*r*
or·gan·iza·tions	*ogjs*	ours	*rs*
or·gan·ize	*og*	our·selves	*rsvs*
or·gan·ized	*og-*	out	*ol*
or·gan·izer	*ogr*	outer	*olr*
or·gan·iz·ers	*ogrs*	out·fit	*olfl*
or·gan·iz·ing	*og*	out·let	*olll*
ori·ent	*oreN*	out·lets	*ollls*
ori·en·ta·tion	*oreNy*	out·line	*olln*
ori·ented	*oreN-*	out·lined	*olln-*
ori·gin	*oryn*	out·lines	*ollns*
origi·nal	*orynl*	out·lin·ing	*olln*

out·look	*olc*	over·throw	*Olro*
out·put	*olpl*	over·thrown	*Olrn*
out·side	*olsd*	over·time	*Ol*
out·stand·ing	*olSN*	over·weight	*Oa*
over	*O*	over·whelm	*Ol*
over·all	*Oa*	over·whelm·ing	*Ol*
over·charge	*Ocy*	over·whelm·ingly	*Olil*
over·come	*Ok*	over·work	*Oo*
overdo	*Odu*	owe	*o*
over·draft	*Odrfl*	owed	*o -*
over·due	*Odu*	own	*O*
over·ex·pen·di·ture	*OxpNCr*	owned	*O -*
over·head	*Ohd*	owner	*or*
over·lay	*Ola*	own·ers	*ors*
over·look	*Olc*	own·er·ship	*orst*
over·looked	*Olc-*	own·ing	*o*
overly	*Ol*	owns	*ov*
over·night	*Oni*		
over·paid	*Opd*		**P**
over·pay·ment	*Opam*		
over·rid·ing	*Ord*	pace	*ps*
over·seas	*Oses*	pack	*pc*
over·sight	*Osi*	pack·age	*pcy*

pack·aged	*pcj-*	pam·phlets	*p flls*
pack·ages	*pcjs*	pan	*pn*
pack·ag·ing	*pcj-*	pane	*pn*
packed	*pc-*	panel	*pnl*
pack·ers	*pcrs*	pan·els	*pnls*
pack·ets	*pcls*	paper	*ppr*
pack·ing	*pc_*	pa·pers	*pprs*
pad	*pd*	pa·per·work	*ppro*
page	*pj*	par	*pr*
pages	*pjs*	para·graph	*prgrf*
pag·ing	*pj-*	par·al·lel	*prll*
paid	*pd*	par·al·lels	*prlls*
paint	*pN*	par·cel	*prsl*
painted	*pN-*	par·cels	*prsls*
paint·ing	*pN_*	par·don	*prdn*
paint·ings	*pN=*	par·ent	*prN*
paints	*pNs*	par·ent·hood	*prNh*
pair	*pr*	par·ents	*prNs*
pairs	*prs*	par·ish	*prs*
pal·let	*pll*	park	*prc*
pal·lets	*plls*	park·ing	*prc_*
palm	*p⁀*	parks	*prcs*
pam·phlet	*p fll*	park·way	*prca*

Word	Outline	Word	Outline
part	*pt*	pas·sage	*psj*
parted	*pt-*	pass·book	*psbc*
par·tial	*prsl*	passed	*ps-*
par·tici·pant	*ppN*	pas·sen·ger	*psnjr*
par·tici·pants	*ppNs*	pas·sen·gers	*psnjrs*
par·tici·pate	*pp*	passes	*pss*
par·tici·pated	*pp-*	pass·ing	*ps_*
par·tici·pates	*pps*	pass·port	*pspl*
par·tici·pat·ing	*pp_*	past	*ps*
par·tici·pa·tion	*ppj*	pas·ture	*psCr*
par·ti·cle	*ptcl*	paths	*pts*
par·ticu·lar	*ptc*	pa·tience	*psN*
par·ticu·larly	*ptcl*	pa·tient	*psN*
par·ticu·lars	*ptcs*	pa·tients	*psNs*
par·ties	*ples*	patio	*plo*
part·ing	*pt_*	pa·tron·age	*plrnj*
partly	*pll*	pat·tern	*plrn*
part·ner	*plnr*	pat·terns	*plrns*
part·ners	*plnrs*	pav·ing	*pv_*
part·ner·ship	*plnrs*	pay	*pa*
parts	*pts*	pay·able	*paB*
party	*ple*	pay·ing	*pa_*
pass	*ps*	pay·ment	*pam*

pay·ments	*pams*	per·form	*Pf*
pay·roll	*parl*	per·form·ance	*PfM*
pays	*pas*	per·formed	*Pf-*
peace	*ps*	per·form·ing	*Pf_*
peak	*pc*	per·haps	*Ph*
pen	*pn*	pe·riod	*pred*
pen·alty	*pnlle*	pe·ri·odic	*predc*
pen·cil	*pNl*	pe·ri·od·ically	*predcll*
pen·cils	*pNls*	pe·ri·od·icals	*predcls*
pend·ing	*pN_*	pe·ri·ods	*preds*
pene·tra·tion	*pnlrj*	per·ma·nent	*PmN*
pen·sion	*pnj*	per·ma·nently	*PmNl*
peo·ple	*ppl*	per·mis·si·ble	*P_sB*
per	*P*	per·mis·sion	*P_j*
per·cent	*%*	per·mit	*P_l*
per·cent·age	*%j*	per·mits	*P_ls*
per·cent·ages	*%js*	per·mit·ted	*P_l-*
per·cen·tile	*%l*	per·mit·ting	*P_l_*
per·cen·tiles	*%ls*	per·sist·ency	*PsSNe*
per·cents	*%s*	per·sist·ent	*PsSN*
per·fect	*Pfc*	per·son	*Psn*
per·fectly	*Pfcl*	per·sonal	*Psnl*
per·fo·rated	*Pfra-*	per·son·al·ities	*Psnl⁶*

per·son·al·ity	*Psnl'*	phrase	*frz*
per·son·al·ized	*Psnlz-*	phys·ical	*fzcl*
per·son·ally	*Psnll*	phys·ically	*fzcll*
per·son·nel	*Psnl*	phy·si·cian	*fzs*
per·sons	*Psns*	phy·si·cians	*fzjs*
per·spec·tive	*Pspcv*	phys·ics	*fzcs*
per·tain·ing	*Pln*	piano	*peno*
per·ti·nent	*PlnN*	pick	*pc*
pe·ti·tion	*ply*	picked	*pc-*
pe·ti·tions	*plys*	pickup	*pcp*
pe·tro·leum	*plrle*	pic·ture	*pccr*
phase	*fz*	pic·tures	*pccrs*
phases	*fzs*	piece	*ps*
phi·loso·phy	*flsfe*	pieces	*pss*
phone	*fn*	pilot	*pll*
photo	*flo*	pin	*pn*
pho·to·cop·ies	*flocpes*	pine	*pn*
pho·to·copy	*flocpe*	pink	*pg*
pho·to·graph	*flogrf*	pins	*pns*
pho·to·graphic	*flogrfc*	pio·neer	*pinr*
pho·to·graphs	*flogrfs*	pipe	*pp*
pho·tos	*flos*	pipe·line	*ppln*
pho·to·stat	*flSt*	pipe·lines	*pplns*

pit·falls	*plfls*	play	*pla*
place	*pls*	played	*pla-*
placed	*pls-*	play·ful	*plaf*
place·ment	*plsm*	play·ing	*pla*
place·ments	*plsms*	plays	*plas*
places	*plss*	plaza	*plza*
plac·ing	*pls*	pleas·ant	*plzN*
plain	*pln*	please	*p*
plain·tiff	*plNf*	pleased	*p-*
plan	*pln*	pleases	*ps*
plane	*pln*	pleas·ing	*p-*
plane·tarium	*plntre*	pleas·ure	*plzr*
planned	*pln-*	pleas·ures	*plzrs*
plan·ning	*pln*	pledge	*plf*
plans	*plns*	plenty	*plNe*
plant	*plN*	plugs	*plgs*
plant·ing	*plN*	plumb·ing	*pl-*
plants	*plNs*	plus	*pls*
plas·tic	*plSc*	pneu·matic	*n-lc*
plas·tics	*plScs*	pocket	*pcl*
plate	*pla*	point	*py*
plates	*plas*	pointed	*py-*
plat·form	*plf*	points	*pys*

poles	*pls*	po·si·tion	*pzj*
po·lice	*pls*	po·si·tions	*pzjs*
poli·cies	*plses*	posi·tive	*pzv*
policy	*plse*	pos·ses·sion	*pzj*
poli·cy·hol·der	*plsehldr*	pos·si·bil·ities	*psßls*
poli·cy·hol·ders	*plsehldrs*	pos·si·bil·ity	*psßl*
po·lit·ical	*pltcl*	pos·si·ble	*psß*
poli·tics	*pltcs*	pos·si·bly	*psß*
poll	*pl*	post	*ps*
pol·lu·tion	*ply*	post·age	*psj*
pool	*pl*	postal	*psl*
pools	*pls*	posted	*ps-*
poor	*pr*	post·ers	*psrs*
popu·lar	*pplr*	post·man	*ps m*
popu·la·tion	*pply*	post·mark	*ps rc*
popu·la·tions	*pplys*	post·paid	*pspd*
port	*pl*	po·ten·tial	*plnsl*
port·able	*plß*	po·ten·tials	*plnsls*
port·fo·lio	*plflo*	poul·try	*pltre*
port·fo·lios	*plflos*	pound	*lb*
por·tion	*pry*	pounds	*lbs*
por·tions	*prys*	pow·der	*podr*
ports	*pls*	power	*por*

pow·ered	*por-*	prepa·ra·tion	*prpry*
pow·ers	*pors*	pre·pare	*Ppr*
prac·ti·cal	*prclcl*	pre·pared	*Ppr-*
prac·ti·cally	*prclcll*	pre·par·ing	*Ppr*
prac·tice	*prcls*	pre·scribe	*PS*
prac·tices	*prclss*	pre·scribed	*PS-*
pray	*pra*	pre·scrip·tion	*PSy*
pre·ced·ing	*Psd*	pres·ence	*pryN*
pre·cious	*prss*	pre·sent (v.)	*p*
pre·cisely	*Pssl*	pres·ent (n.) or (adj.)	*p*
pre·ci·sion	*Psy*	pres·en·ta·tion	*Py*
pre·clude	*Pcld*	pres·en·ta·tions	*Pys*
pre·dict	*Pdc*	pre·sented	*P-*
pre·fer	*Pfr*	pre·sent·ing	*P*
pref·er·able	*prfrB*	pres·ently	*Pl*
pref·er·ably	*prfrB*	pre·sents (v.)	*Ps*
pref·er·ence	*prfrN*	pres·ents (n.)	*Ps*
pre·ferred	*Pfr-*	presi·dent	*P*
pre·limi·nary	*Plmre*	presi·den·tial	*Psl*
prem·ises	*pr ss*	presi·dents	*Ps*
pre·mium	*Pe*	press	*prs*
pre·mi·ums	*Pes*	pressed	*prs-*
pre·paid	*Ppd*	presses	*prss*

press·ing	*prs*	prin·ci·ples	*prNpls*
pres·sure	*prsr*	print	*prN*
pres·sures	*prsrs*	printed	*prN-*
pre·sum·ably	*PzB*	printer	*prNr*
pre·sume	*Pz*	print·ing	*prN*
pre·sump·tion	*Pzy*	prints	*prNs*
pretty	*prte*	prior	*prir*
pre·vent	*PvN*	pri·or·ities	*prir^s*
pre·ven·tion	*Pvny*	pri·or·ity	*prir^i*
pre·view	*Pvu*	pri·vate	*prvt*
pre·vi·ous	*Pves*	privi·lege	*prvl*
pre·vi·ously	*Pvesl*	privi·leged	*prvl-*
price	*prs*	privi·leges	*prvls*
priced	*prs-*	prize	*prz*
prices	*prss*	prizes	*przs*
pric·ing	*prs*	prob·abil·ity	*Pbl^l*
pride	*prd*	prob·able	*Pb*
pri·ma·rily	*prvl*	prob·ably	*Pb*
pri·mary	*prre*	pro·bate	*Pba*
prime	*pr*	prob·lem	*Pbl*
prin·ci·pal	*prNpl*	prob·lems	*Pbls*
prin·ci·pals	*prNpls*	pro·ce·dure	*Psjr*
prin·ci·ple	*prNpl*	pro·ce·dures	*Psjrs*

pro·ceed	*Psd*	pro·fes·sion·als	*Pfjls*
pro·ceed·ing	*Psd*	pro·fes·sor	*Pfsr*
pro·ceed·ings	*Psd*	pro·fi·ciency	*Pfsne*
pro·ceeds	*Psds*	profit	*Pfl*
pro·cess (v.)	*Pss*	prof·it·able	*PflB*
proc·ess (n.)	*Pss*	prof·its	*Pfls*
proc·essed	*Pss-*	pro·gram	*Pg*
pro·cesses (v.)	*Psss*	pro·grammed	*Pg-*
proc·esses (n.)	*Psss*	pro·gram·ming	*Pg_*
proc·ess·ing	*Pss_*	pro·grams	*Pgs*
pro·cure·ment	*Pcrm*	pro·gress (v.)	*Pgrs*
pro·duce	*Pds*	prog·ress (n.)	*Pgrs*
pro·duced	*Pds-*	pro·gres·sive	*Pgrsv*
pro·ducer	*Pdsr*	pro·hibit	*Phbl*
pro·duc·ers	*Pdsrs*	pro·ject (v.)	*Pjc*
pro·duc·ing	*Pds_*	proj·ect (n.)	*Pjc*
prod·uct	*Pdc*	pro·jected	*Pjc-*
pro·duc·tion	*Pdcy*	pro·jec·tion	*Pjcy*
pro·duc·tive	*Pdcv*	pro·jec·tions	*Pjcys*
pro·duc·tiv·ity	*Pdcv^l*	pro·jec·tor	*Pjcr*
prod·ucts	*Pdcs*	pro·jec·tors	*Pjcrs*
pro·fes·sion	*Pff*	pro·jects (v.)	*Pjcs*
pro·fes·sional	*Pfjl*	proj·ects (n.)	*Pjcs*

Word	Shorthand	Word	Shorthand
prom·ise	*P⌢s*	pro·posed	*Ppz-*
prom·ised	*P⌢s-*	propo·si·tion	*Ppzy*
prom·ises	*P⌢ss*	pro·rated	*Pra-*
prom·is·ing	*P⌢s̲*	pros·pect	*Pspc*
pro·mote	*P⌢o*	pro·spec·tive	*Pspcv*
pro·moted	*P⌢o-*	pros·pects	*Pspcs*
pro·mot·ing	*P⌢o̲*	pro·tect	*Plc*
pro·mo·tion	*P⌢y*	pro·tected	*Plc-*
pro·mo·tional	*P⌢yl*	pro·tect·ing	*Plc̲*
pro·mo·tions	*P⌢ys*	pro·tec·tion	*Plcy*
prompt	*P⌢l*	pro·tec·tive	*Plcv*
promptly	*P⌢ll*	pro·to·type	*Pllp*
prompt·ness	*P⌢l'*	proud	*prod*
proof	*prf*	prove	*pv*
proofs	*prfs*	proved	*pv-*
proper	*Ppr*	proven	*pvn*
prop·erly	*Pprl*	proves	*pvs*
prop·er·ties	*prps*	pro·vide	*Pvd*
prop·erty	*prp*	pro·vided	*Pvd-*
pro·por·tion	*Ppry*	provi·dence	*PvdN*
pro·posal	*Ppzl*	pro·vides	*Pvds*
pro·pos·als	*Ppzls*	pro·vid·ing	*Pvd̲*
pro·pose	*Ppz*	prov·ince	*PvN*

pro·vin·cial	*Pvnsl*	pur·chas·ing	*PCs*
prov·ing	*pv*	pure	*pr*
pro·vi·sion	*Pvj*	pur·pose	*Pps*
pro·vi·sions	*Pvjs*	pur·poses	*Ppss*
psy·chi·at·ric	*scelrc*	pur·su·ant	*PsuN*
psy·chology	*sclje*	pur·sue	*Psu*
pub·lic	*pb*	pur·su·ing	*Psu*
pub·li·ca·tion	*pbj*	put	*pl*
pub·li·ca·tions	*pbjs*	put·ting	*pl*
pub·lic·ity	*pbls*		
pub·lish	*pbls*	**Q**	
pub·lished	*pbls-*		
pub·lish·ers	*pblsrs*	quad·ru·pli·cate	*qdrplcl*
pub·lish·ing	*pbls*	quail	*ql*
pump	*p~p*	quali·fi·ca·tion	*qlfj*
pumps	*p~ps*	quali·fi·ca·tions	*qlfjs*
punch	*pnC*	quali·fied	*qlf-*
pu·pils	*ppls*	qualify	*qlf*
pur·chase	*PCs*	qual·ity	*ql*
pur·chased	*PCs-*	quan·ti·ties	*qNls*
pur·chaser	*PCsr*	quan·tity	*qNl*
pur·chas·ers	*PCsrs*	quart	*ql*
pur·chases	*PCss*	quar·ter	*qlr*

quar·ter·back	*qtrbc*	quoted	*qo-*
quar·tered	*qtr-*	quot·ing	*qo̠*
quar·ter·ing	*qtr̠*		
quar·ter·lies	*qtrls*	**R**	
quar·terly	*qtrl*		
quar·ters	*qtrs*	race	*rs*
quarts	*qts*	rack	*rc*
ques·tion	*q*	racks	*rcs*
ques·tion·able	*qß*	ra·dia·tion	*rdej*
ques·tioned	*q-*	radio	*rdo*
ques·tion·ing	*q̠-*	ra·dius	*rdes*
ques·tion·naire	*qr*	rail	*rl*
ques·tion·naires	*qrs*	rail·road	*rlrd*
ques·tions	*qs*	rail·roads	*rlrds*
quick	*qc*	rail·way	*rl a*
quickly	*qcl*	rain	*rn*
quiet	*qil*	raise	*rz*
quite	*qi*	raised	*rz-*
quota	*qta*	rais·ing	*rz̠-*
quo·tas	*qtas*	ran	*rn*
quo·ta·tion	*qtj*	ranch	*rnC*
quo·ta·tions	*qtjs*	ran·dom	*rM*
quote	*qo*	range	*rnj*

Word	Outline	Word	Outline
ranged		read	
ranges		read·able	
rang·ing		reader	
rank		read·ers	
rapid		readily	
rap·idly		read·ing	
rap·ids		read·ings	
rare		re·ad·mit	
rarely		reads	
rate		ready	
rated		real	
rates		re·al·is·tic	
rather		re·al·ize	
rat·ing		re·al·ized	
ratio		really	
raw		re·alty	
reach		rear	
reached		rea·son	
reaches		rea·son·able	
reach·ing		rea·son·ably	
re·ac·tion		rea·son·ing	
re·ac·tions		rea·sons	
re·ac·tor		re·bate	

re·call	*rcl*	re·cord (v.)	*rec*
re·ceipt	*rse*	rec·ord (n.)	*rec*
re·ceipts	*rses*	re·corded	*rec-*
re·ceive	*rsv*	re·corder	*recr*
re·ceived	*rsv-*	re·cord·ing	*rec_*
re·ceives	*rsvo*	re·cords (v.)	*recs*
re·ceiv·ing	*rsv_*	rec·ords (n.)	*recs*
re·cent	*rsN*	re·cover	*rcvr*
re·cently	*rsNl*	re·cov·ered	*rcvr-*
re·cep·tion	*rspj*	re·cov·ery	*rcvre*
reci·pes	*rspes*	rec·rea·tion	*rcrej*
re·cipi·ent	*rspeN*	rec·rea·tional	*rcrejl*
re·cipi·ents	*rspeNs*	re·cruit·ing	*rcru_*
rec·og·ni·tion	*rcgnj*	red	*rd*
rec·og·nize	*rcgnz*	re·deemed	*rd-*
rec·og·nized	*rcgnz-*	re·duce	*rds*
rec·og·niz·ing	*rcgnz_*	re·duced	*rds-*
rec·om·mend	*rcm*	re·duces	*rdss*
rec·om·men·da·tion	*rcmj*	re·duc·ing	*rds_*
rec·om·men·da·tions	*rcmjs*	re·duc·tion	*rdcj*
rec·om·mended	*rcm-*	re·duc·tions	*rdcjs*
rec·om·mend·ing	*rcm_*	refer	*rf*
rec·om·mends	*rcms*	ref·er·ence	*rfN*

ref·er·enced	*rfN-*	re·gional	*rjnl*
ref·er·ences	*rfNs*	re·gions	*rjns*
re·fer·ral	*rfl*	reg·is·ter	*rjSr*
re·fer·rals	*rfls*	reg·is·tered	*rjSr-*
re·ferred	*rf-*	reg·is·ters	*rjSrs*
re·fer·ring	*rf,*	reg·is·tra·tion	*rjSrj*
re·fers	*rfs*	re·gret	*rgrl*
re·fin·ing	*rfn*	re·gret·fully	*rgrlfl*
re·flect	*rflc*	regu·lar	*rglr*
re·flected	*rflc-*	regu·larly	*rglrl*
re·flects	*rflcs*	regu·late	*rgla*
re·form	*rf*	regu·la·tion	*rglj*
re·fund	*rfN*	regu·la·tions	*rgljs*
re·funded	*rfN-*	re·ha·bili·ta·tion	*rhbll*
re·funds	*rfNs*	re·im·burse	*r brs*
re·fuse	*rfz*	re·im·bursed	*r brs-*
re·fused	*rfz-*	re·im·burse·ment	*r brsm*
re·gard	*re*	re·in·forced	*rnfs-*
re·garded	*re-*	re·in·state	*rnSa*
re·gard·ing	*re*	re·in·stated	*rnSa-*
re·gard·less	*rels*	re·in·state·ment	*rnSam*
re·gards	*res*	re·in·sur·ance	*rens*
re·gion	*rjn*	re·it·er·ate	*rilra*

Word	Shorthand	Word	Shorthand
re·ject	*rjc*	re·lo·ca·tion	*rlcy*
re·jected	*rjc-*	re·luc·tant	*rlclN*
re·jec·tion	*rjcy*	rely	*rli*
re·late	*rla*	re·main	*r∾n*
re·lated	*rla-*	re·main·der	*r∾Nr*
re·lates	*rlas*	re·mained	*r∾n-*
re·lat·ing	*rla_*	re·main·ing	*r∾n_*
re·la·tion	*rly*	re·mains	*r∾ns*
re·la·tions	*rlys*	re·mark·able	*r∾rcB*
re·la·tion·ship	*rlyʃ*	re·marks	*r∾rcs*
re·la·tion·ships	*rlyʃs*	remedy	*r∾de*
rela·tive	*rlv*	re·mem·ber	*rmbr*
rela·tively	*rlvl*	re·mind	*rm*
relay	*rla*	re·minded	*rm-*
re·lease	*rls*	re·minder	*rmr*
re·leased	*rls-*	re·mind·ers	*rmrs*
re·leases	*rlss*	re·mit·tance	*r∾lN*
rele·vant	*rlvN*	re·mit·ted	*r∾l-*
re·li·able	*rliB*	re·mit·ting	*r∾l_*
re·lief	*rlf*	re·moval	*r∾vl*
re·lieved	*rlv-*	re·move	*r∾v*
re·lig·ion	*rlyn*	re·moved	*r∾v-*
re·lig·ious	*rlys*	re·mov·ing	*r∾v_*

Word	Shorthand	Word	Shorthand
ren·dered		re·placed	
ren·der·ing		re·place·ment	
renew		re·place·ments	
re·newal		re·plac·ing	
re·newed		re·plies	
rent		reply	
rental		re·ply·ing	
rent·als		re·port	
rent·ing		re·ported	
re·or·der		re·port·edly	
re·or·dered		re·porter	
re·or·gan·iza·tion		re·port·ers	
re·or·gan·ize		re·port·ing	
re·or·gan·ized		re·ports	
re·or·gan·izes		rep·re·sent	
re·or·gan·iz·ing		rep·re·sen·ta·tion	
re·pair		rep·re·sen·ta·tive	
re·paired		rep·re·sen·ta·tives	
re·pair·ing		rep·re·sented	
re·pairs		rep·re·sent·ing	
re·pay·ment		rep·re·sents	
re·peat		re·print	
re·place		re·prints	

Word	Shorthand	Word	Shorthand
re·pro·duce	*rᵖds*	res·er·va·tions	*rzrvjs*
re·pro·duc·tion	*rᵖdcy*	re·serve	*rzrv*
re·prove	*rpv*	re·served	*rzrv-*
re·proved	*rpv-*	re·serves	*rzrvs*
re·proves	*rpvs*	resi·dence	*rzdN*
re·prov·ing	*rpv̄*	resi·dency	*rzdNe*
repu·ta·tion	*rply*	resi·dent	*rzdN*
re·quest	*rqs*	resi·den·tial	*rzdnsl*
re·quested	*rqs-*	resi·dents	*rzdNs*
re·quest·ing	*rqs̄*	res·ig·na·tion	*rzgny*
re·quests	*rqŝs*	re·sis·tance	*rzSN*
re·quire	*rq*	reso·lu·tion	*rzly*
re·quired	*rq-*	reso·lu·tions	*rzlys*
re·quire·ment	*rqm*	re·solve	*rzlv*
re·quire·ments	*rqms*	re·solved	*rzlv-*
re·quires	*rqs*	re·source	*rsrs*
re·quir·ing	*rq̠*	re·sources	*rsrss*
req·ui·si·tion	*rqzy*	re·spect	*rspc*
req·ui·si·tions	*rqzjs*	re·spected	*rspc-*
re·sale	*rsl*	re·spect·fully	*rspcfl*
re·sched·ule	*rscjl*	re·spec·tive	*rspcv*
re·search	*rsC*	re·spec·tively	*rspcvl*
res·er·va·tion	*rzrvy*	re·spects	*rspcs*

re·spond	_rsp_	re·tail·ers	_rtlrs_
re·sponded	_rsp-_	re·tain	_rtn_
re·spond·ing	_rsp_	re·tained	_rtn-_
re·sponds	_rsps_	re·tain·ing	_rtn_
re·sponse	_rsp_	re·tard·ing	_rtrd_
re·spon·si·bil·ities	_rspß⁶_	re·ten·tion	_rtnj_
re·spon·si·bil·ity	_rspß'_	re·tire	_rtr_
re·spon·si·ble	_rspß_	re·tired	_rtr-_
re·spon·sive	_rspv_	re·tire·ment	_rtrm_
rest	_rß_	re·turn	_ret_
res·tau·rant	_rSrN_	re·turned	_ret-_
res·to·ra·tion	_rSrj_	re·turn·ing	_ret_
re·store	_rSr_	re·turns	_rets_
re·strict	_rSrc_	re·veal	_rvl_
re·stricted	_rSrc-_	re·vealed	_rvl-_
re·stric·tions	_rSrcjs_	reve·nue	_rvnu_
re·sult	_rzll_	reve·nues	_rvnus_
re·sulted	_rzll-_	re·verse	_rvrs_
re·sult·ing	_rzll_	re·view	_rvu_
re·sults	_rzlls_	re·viewed	_rvu-_
re·sume	_rz_	re·view·ing	_rvu_
resumé	_rza_	re·views	_rvus_
re·tail	_rtl_	re·vised	_rvz-_

Word	Outline	Word	Outline
re·vi·sion	*rvj*	rock	*rc*
re·vi·sions	*rvjs*	rocket	*rct*
revo·lu·tion	*rvlj*	rocky	*rce*
revo·lu·tion·ary	*rvljre*	rodeo	*rdo*
re·ward	*rw*	role	*rl*
re·ward·ing	*rw*	roll	*rl*
re·writ·ten	*rrtn*	rolled	*rl-*
rib·bon	*rbn*	rolls	*rls*
rib·bons	*rbns*	roof	*rf*
rich	*rC*	room	*r*
rider	*rdr*	rooms	*r_s*
right	*rt*	rose	*rz*
rights	*rts*	ro·tary	*rtre*
rigid	*rjd*	rough	*rf*
ring	*rq*	round	*roN*
rings	*rqs*	route	*ru* N.V. *rot* N.V.
rise	*rz*	routes	*rus*
ris·ing	*rz-*	rou·tine	*rtn*
risk	*rsc*	rout·ing	*ru* N.V. *rot* N.V.
risks	*rscs*	row	*ro*
river	*rvr*	roy·alty	*rylte*
road	*rd*	rub·ber	*rbr*
roads	*rds*	rug	*rq*

rule	*rl*	sale·able	*slß*
rules	*rls*	sales	*sls*
rul·ing	*rl*	sales·man	*sls m*
run	*rn*	sales·man·ship	*slsms*
run·ning	*rn*	sales·men	*slsm*
runs	*rns*	sales·per·son	*slsPsn*
rup·ture	*rpCr*	sales·woman	*sls m*
rush	*rʃ*	sales·women	*sls m*
rust	*rS*	salt	*sll*
		same	*s*

S

		sam·ple	*sa*
		sam·ples	*sa s*
safe	*sf*	sand	*sN*
safely	*sfl*	sand·wich	*sNC*
safety	*sfle*	sani·tary	*sntre*
said	*sd*	sat·is·fac·tion	*saʃ*
sail·ing	*sl*	sat·is·fac·to·rily	*satl*
saint	*sN*	sat·is·fac·tory	*sat*
sake	*sc*	sat·is·fied	*sat-*
sala·ried	*slre-*	sat·is·fies	*sats*
sala·ries	*slres*	sat·isfy	*sat*
salary	*slre*	sat·is·fy·ing	*sat*
sale	*sl*	save	*sv*

Word	Shorthand	Word	Shorthand
saved	*sv-*	sci·en·tific	*sinlfc*
saves	*svs*	scope	*scp*
sav·ing	*sv̠*	score	*scr*
sav·ings	*sv̠̠*	scores	*scrs*
saw	*sa*	scotch	*scl*
say	*sa*	screen	*scrn*
say·ing	*sa̠*	screens	*scrns*
say·ings	*sa̠̠*	script	*S*
says	*sz*	scripts	*Ss*
scale	*scl*	sea	*se*
scan·ning	*scn̠*	seal	*sl*
scat·tered	*sclr-*	seals	*sls*
scene	*sn*	sea·port	*sepl*
sched·ule	*scjl*	sea·ports	*sepls*
sched·uled	*scjl-*	search	*SC*
sched·ules	*scjls*	sea·side	*sesd*
sched·ul·ing	*scjl̠*	sea·son	*szn*
schol·ar·ship	*sclrs*	sea·sonal	*sznl*
schol·ar·ships	*sclrss*	sea·sons	*szns*
school	*scl*	seat	*se*
schools	*scls*	seats	*ses*
sci·ence	*siM*	sec·ond	*sec 2d*
sci·ences	*siMs*	sec·on·dary	*secre*

Word	Outline	Word	Outline
sec·onded	*sec -*	seemed	*s- *
sec·ond·hand	*sechN*	seems	*srs*
sec·ond·ing	*sec̲*	seen	*sn*
sec·ondly	*secl*	sel·dom	*sld*
sec·onds	*secs*	se·lect	*slc*
sec·re·tarial	*secl*	se·lected	*slc -*
sec·re·tar·ies	*secs*	se·lect·ing	*slc̲*
sec·re·tary	*sec*	se·lec·tion	*slcy*
sec·tion	*scy*	se·lec·tions	*slcys*
sec·tions	*scys*	se·lec·tive	*slcv*
sec·tor	*scr*	self	*sf*
se·cure	*scr*	self-addressed	*sfadrs-*
se·cured	*scr -*	self-assurance	*sfasrN*
se·cur·ing	*scr̲*	self-confidence	*sfkfdN*
se·cu·ri·ties	*scr⁻ᵗˢ*	self-defense	*sfdfN*
se·cu·rity	*scrˡ*	self-explanatory	*sfxplnlre*
see	*se*	self-improvement	*sf pvm*
seed	*sd*	self-made	*sfd*
see·ing	*se̲*	sell	*sl*
seek	*sc*	sell·ers	*slrs*
seek·ing	*sc̲*	sell·ing	*sl̲*
seeks	*scs*	sells	*sls*
seem	*s*	se·mes·ter	*sSr*

word	shorthand	word	shorthand
semi·nar	*smr*	ser·mon	*Sm*
semi·nars	*smrs*	serve	*Sv*
sen·ate	*snt*	served	*Sv-*
sena·tor	*sntr*	serves	*Svs*
sena·tors	*sntrs*	serv·ice	*Svs*
send	*sN*	serv·ice·man	*Svs—m*
send·ing	*sN_*	serv·ice·men	*Svsm*
sen·ior	*sr*	serv·ices	*Svss*
sen·ior·ity	*sr^l*	serv·ice·woman	*Svs—m*
sen·iors	*srs*	serv·ice·women	*Svsm*
sense	*sN*	serv·ing	*Sv_*
senses	*sNs*	ses·sion	*sj*
sen·si·tive	*sNv*	ses·sions	*sjs*
sent	*sN*	set	*st*
sen·tence	*sNN*	sets	*sts*
sepa·rate	v. *spra* adj. *sprt*	set·ting	*st_*
sepa·rately	*sprtl*	set·tle	*stl*
sepa·ra·tion	*sprj*	set·tled	*stl-*
se·quen·tial	*sqnst*	set·tle·ment	*stlm*
se·rial	*srel*	set·tle·ments	*stlms*
se·ries	*srz*	sev·eral	*sv*
se·ri·ous	*sres*	se·vere	*svr*
se·ri·ously	*sresl*	se·verely	*svrl*

sewer	*sur*	shifts	*sfls*
shade	*sd*	ship	*s*
shaft	*sfl*	ship·ment	*sm*
shall	*sl*	ship·ments	*sms*
shape	*sp*	shipped	*s-*
shapes	*sps*	ship·per	*sr*
share	*sr*	ship·pers	*srs*
shared	*sr-*	ship·ping	*s_*
share·holder	*srhldr*	ships	*ss*
share·hold·ers	*srhldrs*	ship·yards	*syds*
shares	*srs*	shirts	*srts*
shar·ing	*sr_*	shocked	*sc-*
sharp	*srp*	shoe	*su*
sharply	*srpl*	shoes	*sus*
she	*se*	shoot	*su*
sheep	*sp*	shoot·ing	*su_*
sheet	*se*	shop	*sp*
sheets	*ses*	shop·ping	*sp_*
shelf	*slf*	shops	*sps*
shell	*sl*	short	*srt*
shelves	*slvs*	short·age	*srty*
shift	*sfl*	short·ages	*srtys*
shift·ing	*sfl_*	shorter	*srtr*

short·hand	*srthn*	sig·na·ture	*sig*
shortly	*srll*	sig·na·tures	*sigs*
shorts	*srls*	signed	*sn-*
shot	*sl*	sig·nifi·cance	*sig*
should	*sd*	sig·nifi·cant	*sig*
shouldn't	*sdn*	sig·nifi·cantly	*sigl*
show	*so*	sign·ing	*sn*
showed	*so-*	signs	*sns*
shower	*sor*	sili·con	*slk*
show·ing	*so*	sil·ver	*slvr*
show·ings	*so*	simi·lar	*s lr*
shown	*sn*	simi·larly	*s lrl*
shows	*soo*	sim·ple	*s pl*
shut	*sl*	sim·plic·ity	*s pls'*
shut·down	*sldon*	sim·pli·fied	*s plf-*
sick	*sc*	sim·ply	*s pl*
sick·ness	*sc'*	since	*sn*
side	*sd*	sin·cere	*snsr*
sides	*sds*	sin·cerely	*snsrl*
sight	*si*	sin·gle	*sgl*
sign	*sn*	sis·ter	*ssr*
sig·nal	*sgnl*	sis·ters	*ssrs*
sig·nals	*sgnls*	sit	*sl*

site	_si_	slightly	_slil_
sites	_sis_	slip	_slp_
situ·ate	_sil_	slips	_slps_
situ·ated	_sil-_	slow	_slo_
situ·ates	_sils_	small	_sml_
situ·at·ing	_sil_	smaller	_smlr_
situ·ation	_sily_	smocks	_smcs_
situ·ations	_silys_	smoke	_smc_
siz·able	_szб_	smooth	_sml_
size	_sz_	smoothly	_smll_
sized	_sz-_	snow	_sno_
sizes	_szs_	so	_so_
sketch	_scC_	soap	_sp_
ski	_sce_	so·cial	_ssl_
ski·ing	_sce_	so·ci·ety	_ssi_
skill	_scl_	sock	_sc_
skilled	_scl-_	sod	_sd_
skills	_scls_	soft	_sfl_
slab	_slb_	soil	_syl_
slacks	_slcs_	soils	_syls_
sleeves	_slvs_	sold	_sld_
slides	_slds_	sole	_sl_
slight	_sli_	solely	_sll_

soles	_sls_	source	_srs_
solid	_sld_	sources	_srss_
so·lu·tion	_sly_	south	_S_
so·lu·tions	_slys_	south·east	_SE_
solve	_slv_	south·east·erly	_SErl_
solved	_slv-_	south·east·ern	_SErn_
sol·vent	_slvn_	south·erly	_Srl_
solv·ing	_slv_	south·ern	_Srn_
some	_s_	south·ward	_Sw_
some·body	_s bde_	south·west	_SW_
some·one	_s ı_	south·west·ern	_SWrn_
some·thing	_s_	space	_sps_
some·time	_s t_	spaces	_spss_
some·times	_s ts_	spac·ing	_sps_
some·what	_s t_	spank	_spq_
some·where	_s r_	spare	_spr_
son	_sn_	sparks	_sprcs_
sons	_sns_	speak	_spc_
soon	_sn_	speaker	_spcr_
sooner	_snr_	speak·ers	_spcrs_
sorry	_sre_	speak·ing	_spc_
sort	_srl_	speaks	_spcs_
sound	_son_	spe·cial	_spsl_

Word	Shorthand	Word	Shorthand
spe·cial·ist	*spsls*	splen·did	*splNd*
spe·cial·ists	*spslss*	split	*spll*
spe·cial·ized	*spslz-*	spoke	*spc*
spe·cially	*spsll*	spon·sor	*spNr*
spe·cials	*spsls*	spon·sored	*spNr-*
spe·cialty	*spslle*	spon·sor·ing	*spNr_*
spe·cific	*sp*	spon·sors	*spNrs*
spe·cif·ically	*spl*	spon·sor·ship	*spNrs*
speci·fi·ca·tion	*spf*	spools	*spls*
speci·fi·ca·tions	*spfs*	sport	*spl*
speci·fied	*sp-*	sports	*spls*
speci·fies	*sps*	spot	*spl*
specify	*sp*	spots	*spls*
speci·fy·ing	*sp_*	spouse	*spos*
speci·men	*spsm*	spray	*spra*
speech	*spC*	spread	*sprd*
speed	*spd*	spree	*spre*
speeds	*spds*	spring	*sprq*
spend	*spN*	springs	*sprqs*
spend·ing	*spN_*	sprin·kler	*sprqlr*
spent	*spN*	sprocket	*sprcl*
spirit	*sprl*	sprock·ets	*sprcls*
spite	*spi*	square	*sq*

squared	_sq-_	stan·dard·ized	_Sdz-_
squares	_sqs_	stan·dard·izes	_Sdzs_
squar·est	_sqs_	stan·dard·iz·ing	_Sdz-_
squar·ing	_sq-_	stan·dards	_Sds_
sta·bil·ity	_SSı_	stand·ing	_SN_
sta·ble	_SS_	stand·point	_SNpy_
stack	_Sc_	stands	_SNs_
staff	_Sf_	sta·ples	_Spls_
staffed	_Sf-_	star·board	_Srbrd_
staff·ing	_Sf-_	stars	_Srs_
staffs	_Sfs_	start	_Srt_
stage	_Sy_	started	_Srt-_
stages	_Sys_	starter	_Srtr_
stain·less	_Snls_	start·ing	_Srt-_
stake	_Sc_	starts	_Srts_
stamp	_Sp_	state	_Sa_
stamped	_Sp-_	stated	_Sa-_
stamp·ing	_Sp-_	state·ment	_Sam_
stamps	_Sps_	state·ments	_Sams_
stand	_SN_	states	_Sas_
stan·dard	_Sd_	static	_Stc_
stan·dard·iza·tion	_Sdy_	stat·ing	_Sa-_
stan·dard·ize	_Sdz_	sta·tion	_Sy_

Word	Outline	Word	Outline
sta·tioner	*Syr*	steps	*Sps*
sta·tion·ery	*Syre*	ster·ling	*Srlg*
sta·tions	*Sys*	stew·ard·ess	*Sws*
sta·tis·tic	*StSc*	stew·ard·ship	*Sws*
sta·tis·ti·cal	*StScl*	sticker	*Scr*
sta·tis·tics	*StScs*	still	*Sl*
status	*Sts*	stimu·late	*S la*
statue	*SCu*	stimu·lat·ing	*S la*
stat·utes	*SCus*	sti·pend	*SpN*
stay	*Sa*	stipu·lated	*Spla-*
stay·ing	*Sa*	stock	*Sc*
steadily	*Sdl*	stock·hold·ers	*Schldrs*
steady	*Sde*	stock·ing	*Sc*
steam	*S*	stock·pile	*Scpl*
steam·ship	*S*	stocks	*Scs*
steel	*Sl*	stock·yards	*Scyds*
steer·ing	*Sr*	stop	*Sp*
stem	*S*	stop·ping	*Sp*
sten·cil	*SNl*	stor·age	*Srj*
sten·cil·ing	*SNl*	store	*Sr*
sten·cils	*SNls*	stored	*Sr-*
ste·nog·ra·phers	*Sngrfrs*	stores	*Srs*
step	*Sp*	sto·ries	*Sres*

story		stu·dents	
straight		stud·ied	
straighten		stud·ies	
stream		study	
street		study·ing	
street·car		style	
streets		styled	
strength		styles	
strengthen		sub·com·mit·tee	
stress		sub·com·mit·tees	
strict		sub·con·scious	
strictly		sub·di·vi·sion	
strike		sub·ject	
strip		sub·jects	
strips		sub·ma·rine	
strive		sub·mis·sion	
strong		sub·mit	
strongly		sub·mit·ted	
struc·tural		sub·mit·ting	
struc·ture		sub·scribe	
struc·tures		sub·scriber	
stub		sub·scrib·ers	
stu·dent		sub·scribes	

Word	Shorthand	Word	Shorthand
sub·scrib·ing	sS	suf·fi·cient	sfsN
sub·scrip·tion	sSj	suf·fi·ciently	sfsNl
sub·scrip·tions	sSjs	sugar	sgr
sub·se·quent	ssqN	sug·gest	sug
sub·se·quently	ssqNl	sug·gested	sug-
sub·sidi·ar·ies	ssderes	sug·gest·ing	sug-
sub·sidi·ary	ssdere	sug·ges·tion	sugj
sub·sis·tence	ssSN	sug·ges·tions	sugjs
sub·stan·dard	sSd	sug·gests	sugs
sub·stan·tial	sSnsl	suit	su
sub·stan·tially	sSnsll	suit·abil·ity	subl
sub·stan·ti·ate	sSnsa	suit·able	sub
sub·sti·tute	sSlu	suited	su-
sub·urbs	srbs	suits	sus
suc·ceed	scsd	sum	s
suc·cess	suc	sum·ma·ries	s·res
suc·cesses	sucs	sum·mary	s·re
suc·cess·ful	sucf	sum·mer	s·r
suc·cess·fully	sucfl	sum·mons	sms
such	sC	super	S
sud·den	sdn	su·per·in·ten·dent	S
sud·denly	sdnl	su·per·in·ten·dents	Ss
suf·fered	sfr-	su·pe·rior	sprer

Word	Shorthand	Word	Shorthand
su·per·mar·ket	_S_	sup·pose	_spz_
su·per·vise	_Svz_	sup·posed	_spz-_
su·per·vised	_Svz-_	su·preme	_spr_
su·per·vis·ing	_Svz_	sur·charge	_SG_
su·per·vi·sion	_Sv٦_	sure	_sr_
su·per·vi·sor	_Svzr_	surely	_srl_
su·per·vi·sors	_Svzrs_	sur·face	_Sfs_
su·per·vi·sory	_Svzre_	sur·faces	_Sfss_
sup·ple·ment	_splm_	sur·geon	_Sjn_
sup·ple·men·tal	_splml_	sur·gery	_Sjre_
sup·ple·men·tary	_splmre_	sur·gi·cal	_Sjcl_
sup·ple·ments	_splms_	sur·plus	_Spls_
sup·plied	_spli-_	sur·pluses	_Splss_
sup·plier	_splir_	sur·prise	_Sprz_
sup·pli·ers	_splirs_	sur·prised	_Sprz-_
sup·plies	_splis_	sur·ren·der	_SNr_
sup·ply	_spli_	sur·round	_SoN_
sup·ply·ing	_spli_	sur·round·ing	_SoN_
sup·port	_spt_	sur·vey	_Sva_
sup·ported	_spt-_	sur·veyor	_Svar_
sup·porter	_sptr_	sur·veys	_Svas_
sup·port·ing	_spt_	sur·viv·ing	_Svv_
sup·ports	_spts_	sus·pect	_sspc_

Word	Shorthand	Word	Shorthand
sus·pense	*sspN*	take	*lc*
sus·pen·sion	*sspny*	taken	*lcn*
sus·tained	*sSn-*	takes	*lcs*
sweep·stakes	*s pScs*	tak·ing	*lc*
switch	*s C*	tal·ent	*lLn*
switches	*s Cs*	tal·ents	*lLns*
switch·ing	*s C*	talk	*lc*
sym·bol	*s B*	talked	*lc-*
sym·pa·thetic	*s pLLc*	talk·ing	*lc*
sym·pa·thize	*s plz*	talks	*lcs*
sym·pa·thy	*s ple*	tank	*lq*
syn·thetic	*snLLc*	tanks	*lqs*
sys·tem	*sS*	tap	*lp*
sys·tem·atic	*sSlc*	tape	*lp*
sys·tems	*sSs*	tapes	*lps*
		tap·ping	*lp-*
T		tar	*lr*
		tar·iff	*lrf*
		task	*lsc*
table	*lB*	tax	*lx*
ta·bles	*lBs*	tax·able	*lxB*
tag	*lq*	taxa·tion	*lxy*
tags	*lqs*	taxed	*lx-*
tai·lored	*lLr-*		

taxes	*Lxs*	tele·vi·sion	*Uvy*
tax·payer	*Lxpar*	tell	*Ul*
teach	*UC*	tell·ing	*Ul*
teacher	*UCr*	tells	*Uls*
teach·ers	*UCrs*	tem·pera·ture	*LprCr*
teach·ing	*UC*	tem·pera·tures	*LprCrs*
team	*L*	tempo	*Lpo*
tea·pot	*lepl*	tem·po·rarily	*Lprrl*
tear	*lr*	tem·po·rary	*Lprre*
tech·ni·cal	*Lcncl*	ten·ant	*LnN*
tech·ni·cally	*Lcncll*	ten·ants	*LnNs*
tech·ni·cian	*Lcny*	tend	*UN*
tech·ni·cians	*Lcnys*	ten·ta·tive	*UNv*
tech·nique	*Lcnc*	ten·ta·tively	*UNvl*
tech·niques	*Lcncs*	term	*lr*
tech·nology	*Lcnlje*	ter·mi·nal	*Lrml*
teen·age	*Lnaj*	ter·mi·nals	*Lrmls*
teeth	*Ul*	ter·mi·nate	*Lrma*
tele·gram	*Ulg*	ter·mi·nated	*Lrma-*
tele·graph	*Ulgrf*	ter·mi·na·tion	*Lrmy*
tele·phone	*Ulfn*	terms	*Lrs*
tele·phones	*Ulfns*	ter·race	*Lrs*
tele·type	*Ullp*	ter·ri·ble	*LrB*

Word	Shorthand	Word	Shorthand
ter·ri·to·ries	*lrlres*	theirs	*lrs*
ter·ri·tory	*lrlre*	them	*ln*
test	*lS*	theme	*ln*
tested	*lS-*	them·selves	*lnsvs*
tes·ti·fied	*lSf-*	then	*ln*
tes·ti·mony	*lSne*	theory	*lere*
test·ing	*lS*	thera·pist	*lrpS*
tests	*lSs*	therapy	*lrpe*
text	*lxl*	there	*lr*
text·book	*lxlbc*	there·af·ter	*lraf*
text·books	*lxlbcs*	thereby	*lrb*
tex·tile	*lxll*	there·fore	*lrf*
texts	*lxls*	therein	*lrn*
than	*ln*	thereof	*lrv*
thank	*lq*	thereon	*lro*
thank·ing	*lq-*	thereto	*lrl*
thanks	*lqs*	there·to·fore	*lrlf*
that	*la*	ther·mal	*lrl*
that's	*las*	ther·mo·stats	*lrSls*
the	*(*	these	*lz*
thea·ter	*lelr*	they	*ly*
theft	*Yl*	they'll	*lyl*
their	*lr*	they're	*lyr*

Word	Shorthand	Word	Shorthand
they've	*Lyjr*	tidal	*Ldl*
thick	*Lc*	tie	*Li*
thin	*Ln*	tied	*Li-*
thing	*Lq*	tile	*Ll*
things	*Lqs*	time	*L*
think	*Lq*	timely	*Ll*
think·ing	*Lq-*	times	*Ls*
this	*Ls*	time·ta·ble	*L lB*
thor·ough	*Lro*	time·ta·bles	*L lBs*
thor·oughly	*Lrol*	tim·ing	*L-*
those	*Loz*	tip	*Lp*
though	*Lo*	tips	*Lps*
thought	*Ll*	tire	*Lr*
thought·ful	*Llf*	tires	*Lrs*
thoughts	*Lls*	title	*Ll*
thou·sand	*T*	ti·tled	*Ll-*
thou·sands	*Ts*	ti·tles	*Lls*
thou·sandth	*Tl*	to	*L*
through	*Lru*	today	*Ld*
through·out	*Lruol*	to·gether	*Lglr*
thus	*Ls*	token	*Lcn*
ticket	*Lcl*	told	*Lld*
tick·ets	*Lcls*	to·mor·row	*Lro*

Word	Outline	Word	Outline
ton	*ln*	tower	*lor*
ton·nage	*lnj*	town	*lon*
tons	*lns*	town·ship	*lons*
too	*l*	toy	*ly*
took	*lc*	track	*lrc*
tool	*ll*	tracks	*lrcs*
tools	*lls*	tract	*lrc*
tooth	*ll*	trac·tor	*lrclr*
top	*lp*	trade	*lrd*
topic	*lpc*	trad·ing	*lrd*
top·ics	*lpcs*	tra·di·tions	*lrdjs*
total	*lol*	traf·fic	*lrfc*
to·taled	*lol-*	trailer	*lrlr*
to·tal·ing	*lol*	trail·ers	*lrlrs*
to·tally	*loll*	train	*lrn*
to·tals	*lols*	trained	*lrn-*
touch	*lC*	trainee	*lrne*
tough	*lf*	train·ing	*lrn*
tour	*lr*	trains	*lrns*
tour·na·ment	*lrnm*	tran·quil	*Tql*
tours	*lrs*	trans·act	*Tac*
to·ward	*lw*	trans·ac·tion	*Tacj*
to·wards	*lws*	trans·ac·tions	*Tacjs*

Word	Shorthand	Word	Shorthand
tran·scribe	*TS*	trav·el·ing	*lrvl*
tran·script	*TS*	trav·els	*lrvls*
trans·fer	*Tfr*	treas·ure	*lrzr*
trans·ferred	*Tfr-*	treas·urer	*lrzrr*
trans·fer·ring	*Tfr_*	treas·ury	*lrzre*
trans·fers	*Tfrs*	treat	*lre*
trans·former	*Tfr*	treated	*lre-*
trans·form·ers	*Tfrs*	trea·ties	*lrles*
tran·sis·tor	*TSr*	treat·ment	*lrem*
tran·sis·tors	*TSrs*	treaty	*lrle*
tran·sit	*Tl*	tree	*lre*
tran·si·tion	*Tη*	trees	*lres*
trans·la·tion	*Tly*	tre·men·dous	*lrmds*
trans·mis·sion	*Tη*	trend	*lrN*
trans·mit·tal	*Tll*	trends	*lrNs*
trans·plant	*TplN*	trial	*lril*
trans·port	*Tpl*	tri·an·gle	*lrigl*
trans·por·ta·tion	*Tply*	tribu·tar·ies	*lrblres*
trans·ported	*Tpl-*	tried	*lri-*
trans·porter	*Tplr*	trip	*lrp*
trans·port·ing	*Tpl_*	trips	*lrps*
trans·ports	*Tpls*	trouble	*lrB*
travel	*lrvl*	truck	*lrc*

Word	Shorthand	Word	Shorthand
trucks	*lrcs*	type·writ·ing	*lpri*
true	*lru*	typ·ical	*lpcl*
truly	*lrul*	typ·ing	*lp*
trust	*lrS*	typ·ists	*lpSs*
trus·tee	*lrSe*		
trus·tees	*lrSes*	**U**	
trust·ing	*lrS*		
trusts	*lrSs*	ul·ti·mate	*ult_l*
truth	*lrl*	ul·ti·mately	*ult_ll*
try	*lri*	un·able	*uB*
try·ing	*lri*	unani·mously	*unn_sl*
tube	*lb*	un·au·thor·ized	*ualrz-*
tub·ing	*lb*	un·cer·tain	*uStn*
tui·tion	*luy*	un·changed	*uCny-*
turn	*lrn*	under	*U*
turned	*lrn-*	un·der·cur·rent	*UcrN*
turn·ing	*lrn*	un·der·go·ing	*Ug*
turn·over	*lrnO*	un·der·gradu·ate	*Ugryul*
twin	*Ln*	un·der·ground	*UgroN*
type	*lp*	un·der·handed	*UhN-*
typed	*lp-*	un·der·lie·	*Uli*
types	*lps*	un·der·line	*Uln*
type·writer	*lprir*	un·der·lined	*Uln-*

Word	Shorthand	Word	Shorthand
un·der·lines	*Ulns*	un·der·writ·ing	*Uri*
un·der·ly·ing	*Uli*	un·dis·trib·uted	*uD-*
un·der·mine	*Um*	un·di·vided	*udvd-*
un·der·neath	*Unl*	un·doubt·edly	*udotl*
un·der·score	*Uscr*	undue	*udu*
un·der·scored	*Uscr -*	un·earned	*uern-*
un·der·scores	*Uscrs*	un·em·ployed	*u p-*
un·der·scor·ing	*Uscr*	un·em·ploy·ment	*u pm*
un·der·signed	*Usn-*	un·fair	*ufr*
un·der·stand	*USN*	un·for·tu·nate	*ufcnl*
un·der·stand·able	*USNB*	un·for·tu·nately	*ufcnll*
un·der·stand·ably	*USNB*	un·grate·ful	*ugrf*
un·der·stand·ing	*USN*	uni·form	*unf*
un·der·stood	*USd*	uni·for·mity	*unf*
un·der·take	*Ulc*	un·im·por·tant	*u pl*
un·der·taken	*Ulcn*	union	*unyn*
un·der·takes	*Ulcs*	un·ions	*unyns*
un·der·tak·ing	*Ulc*	unique	*unc*
un·der·took	*Ulc*	unit	*unl*
un·der·way	*Ua*	united	*uni-*
un·der·write	*Uri*	units	*unls*
un·der·writer	*Urir*	uni·ver·sal	*unvrsl*
un·der·writ·ers	*Urirs*	uni·ver·si·ties	*Us*

uni·ver·sity	*U*	un·will·ing·ness	*ul'*
un·less	*uls*	up	*p*
un·like	*ulc*	up·dated	*pda-*
un·load·ing	*uld*	upon	*po*
un·nec·es·sarily	*unesl*	upper	*pr*
un·nec·es·sary	*unes*	up·ward	*pw*
un·or·gan·ized	*uog-*	urban	*urbn*
un·paid	*upd*	urge	*ury*
un·prof·it·able	*uflB*	urged	*ury-*
un·rea·son·able	*urznB*	ur·gency	*uryNe*
un·re·spon·sive	*urspv*	ur·gent	*uryN*
un·sat·is·fac·to·rily	*usall*	urg·ing	*ury-*
un·sat·is·fac·tory	*usal*	us	*s*
un·sat·is·fied	*usal-*	usage	*usy*
un·suc·cess·ful	*usucf*	use	*uz ŭs* (v. / n.)
un·suc·cess·fully	*usucfl*	used	*uz-*
until	*ull*	use·ful	*usf*
un·used	*uuz-*	use·less	*usls*
un·usual	*uuz*	user	*uzr*
un·usu·ally	*uuzl*	users	*uzrs*
un·wel·come	*ulk*	uses	*uzš ŭss* (v. / n.)
un·will·ing	*ul-*	using	*uz-*
un·will·ingly	*ulf*	usual	*uz*

usu·ally	*uzl*	val·ued	*vlu-*
util·ities	*ull^ls*	val·ues	*vlus*
util·ity	*ull^l*	valve	*vlv*
util·iza·tion	*ullzy*	valves	*vlvs*
util·ize	*ullz*	van	*vn*
util·ized	*ullz-*	van·dal·ism	*vNlz*
util·iz·ing	*ullz̦*	vapor	*vpr*
ut·most	*ut͜s*	vari·able	*vreß*
		var·ied	*vre-*
		var·ies	*vres*
V		va·ri·eties	*vri^ls*
		va·ri·ety	*vri^l*
		vari·ous	*vres*
va·can·cies	*vcNes*	vary	*vre*
va·cancy	*vcNe*	vast	*vs*
va·cant	*vcN*	ve·hi·cle	*vhcl*
va·ca·tion	*vcy*	ve·hi·cles	*vhcls*
va·ca·tions	*vcys*	ven·dor	*vNr*
vacuum	*vcy*	ven·ture	*vnCr*
valid	*vld*	ver·bal	*vrß*
va·lid·ity	*vld^l*	veri·fi·ca·tion	*vrf*
val·ley	*vle*	veri·fied	*vrf-*
valu·able	*vluß*	verify	*vrf*
valu·ation	*vluy*		
value	*vlu*		

veri·fy·ing	*vrf-*	vir·tu·ally	*vrCull*
ver·sa·til·ity	*vrstl*	visa	*vza*
ver·sion	*vry*	vis·ible	*vzß*
ver·sus	*vrss*	vi·sion	*vy*
ver·ti·cal	*vrtcl*	visit	*vzt*
very	*v*	vis·ited	*vzt-*
ves·sel	*vsl*	vis·it·ing	*vzt_*
ves·sels	*vsls*	visi·tor	*vztr*
vested	*vs-*	visi·tors	*vztrs*
vet·er·ans	*vtrns*	vis·its	*vzts*
vexa·tion	*vxy*	visual	*vzul*
via	*va*	vital	*vtl*
vice	*vo*	vo·ca·tional	*vcyl*
vice presi·dent	*VP*	voice	*vys*
vice presi·den·tial	*VPsl*	volt	*vlt*
vice presi·dents	*VPs*	volt·age	*vlly*
vi·cin·ity	*vsn*	vol·ume	*vol*
view	*vu*	vol·umes	*vols*
view·ers	*vurs*	vol·un·tary	*vlntre*
views	*vus*	vol·un·teer	*vlntr*
vil·lage	*vly*	vol·un·teers	*vlntrs*
vio·la·tion	*vrly*	vote	*vo*
vio·la·tions	*vrlys*	voted	*vo-*

vot·ers	*vors*	war·ranted	*rM-*
voucher	*voCr*	war·ranty	*rMe*
		was	*z*
	W	wash	*A*
		wash·ing	*A*
wage	*y*	wasn't	*zM*
wages	*ys*	waste	*S*
wagon	*gn*	watch	*C*
wait	*a*	watch·ing	*C*
wait·ing	*a*	water	*lr*
waiver	*vr*	wa·ter·ing	*lr*
walk	*c*	wa·ters	*lrs*
wall	*l*	wa·ter·shed	*lrsd*
walls	*ls*	watt	*l*
wal·nut	*lnl*	wax	*x*
want	*M*	way	*a*
wanted	*M-*	ways	*as*
wants	*Ms*	we	*e*
war	*r*	we'd	*e'd*
ward	*w*	we'll	*e'l*
ware·house	*rhos*	we're	*e'r*
warn·ing	*rn*	we've	*e'v*
war·rant	*rM*	wear	*r*

wear·ing	*r*	west	*W*	
weather	*ir*	west·erly	*Wrl*	
weed	*d*	west·ern	*Wrn*	
week	*c*	west·erner	*Wrnr*	
week·end	*cn*	west·ward	*Ww*	
weekly	*cl*	wet	*l*	
weeks	*cs*	what	*l*	
weigh	*a*	what's	*ls*	
weigh·ing	*a̱*	what·ever	*lE*	
weigh·ings	*a̳*	what·so·ever	*lsoE*	
weight	*a*	wheat	*e*	
weights	*as*	wheel	*l*	
wel·come	*lk*	wheels	*ls*	
wel·comed	*lk-*	when	*n*	
wel·comes	*lks*	when·ever	*nE*	
wel·com·ing	*lḵ*	where	*r*	
welded	*ld-*	whereas	*rz*	
weld·ing	*lḏ*	whereby	*rb*	
wel·fare	*lfr*	wherein	*rn*	
well	*l*	wher·ever	*rE*	
wells	*ls*	whether	*lr*	
went	*n*	which	*C*	
were	*_*	which·ever	*CE*	

while	*l*	will·ful	*lf*
white	*i*	will·fully	*lfl*
who	*hu*	will·ing	*l*
who·ever	*huE*	will·ingly	*ll*
whole	*hl*	will·ing·ness	*l'*
whole·heart·edly	*hlhrt-l*	wills	*ls*
whole·sale	*hlsl*	win	*n*
wholly	*hll*	wind	*N*
whom	*h*	win·dow	*No*
whom·ever	*hvE*	win·dows	*Nos*
whose	*hz*	wine	*n*
why	*y*	wing	*q*
wide	*d*	win·ner	*nr*
widely	*dl*	win·ners	*nrs*
wid·en·ing	*dn*	win·ter	*Nr*
wid·est	*ds*	wire	*r*
widow	*do*	wis·dom	*zd*
width	*dl*	wise	*z*
wife	*f*	wish	*s*
wil·der·ness	*lds'*	wished	*s-*
wild·life	*ldlf*	wishes	*ss*
will	*l*	wish·ing	*s-*
willed	*l-*	wit	*l*

Word	Shorthand	Word	Shorthand
with	⌣	won	_n
with·draw	_dra	won't	_n
with·drawal	_dral	won·der	_nr
with·draw·als	_drals	won·der·ful	_nrf
with·draw·ing	_dra_	won·der·ing	_nr_
with·drawn	_drn	wood	_d
with·draws	_dras	wood·lands	_dlns
with·drew	_dru	woods	_ds
with·held	_hld	wool	_l
with·hold	_hld	word	_rd
with·hold·ing	_hld_	word·ing	_rd_
with·hold·ings	_hld_	words	_rds
with·holds	_hlds	work	_o
within	_n	work·book	_obc
with·out	_ot	work·books	_obcs
with·stand	_sn	worked	_o-
with·stand·ing	_sn_	worker	_or
with·stands	_sns	work·ers	_ors
with·stood	_sd	work·ing	_o_
wit·ness	_t'	work·man	_o m
wit·nesses	_t"	work·man·ship	_oms
woman	_m	work·men	_om
women	_m	works	_os

word	shorthand	word	shorthand
work·shop	_osp_		
world	_o_		
worldly	_ol_	yard	_yd_
worlds	_os_	yards	_yds_
worn	_rn_	yard·stick	_ydSc_
worse	_rs_	year	_yr_
worth	_rl_	yearly	_yrl_
worth·while	_rll_	years	_yrs_
wor·thy	_rle_	yel·low	_ylo_
would	_d_	yes	_ys_
wouldn't	_dN_	yes·ter·day	_ySrd_
write	_ru_	yes·ter·days	_ySrds_
writer	_rur_	yet	_yl_
writ·ers	_rurs_	yield	_yld_
writ·ing	_ru_	you	_u_
writ·ten	_rln_	you'd	_u'd_
wrong	_rq_	you'll	_u'l_
wrote	_ro_	you're	_u'r_
		you've	_u'v_

X

word	shorthand	word	shorthand
		young	_yq_
		younger	_ygr_
x-ray	_vra_	young·sters	_ygSrs_
		your	_u_

Y

yours	*us*
your·self	*usf*
your·selves	*usvs*
youth	*ul*

Z

zero	*zro*
zip	*zp*
zone	*zn*
zones	*zns*
zon·ing	*zn*

INDEX OF BRIEF FORMS

ALPHABETICAL LISTING

a (an)	.	as (was)	*3*
able	*B*	associate	*aso*
about	*ab*	at (it)	*/*
accept	*ac*	be (been, but, buy, by)	*b*
accomplish	*ak*	been (be, but, buy, by)	*b*
acknowledge	*acy*	between	*bln*
administrate	*Am*	both	*bo*
advantage	*Avy*	business	*bs*
after	*af*	but (be, been, buy, by)	*b*
again (against)	*aq*	buy (be, been, but, by)	*b*
against (again)	*aq*	by (be, been, but, buy)	*b*
already	*Ar*	came (come, committee)	*k*
always	*a*	can	*c*
am (more)	⌒	character (characteristic)	*crc*
an (a)	.	characteristic (character)	*crc*
appreciate	*ap*	charge	*G*
appropriate	*apo*	circumstance	*Sk*
approximate	*apx*	come (came, committee)	*k*
are (our)	*r*	committee (came, come)	*k*
arrange	*ar*	complete	*kp*

Word	Outline	Word	Outline
congratulate	*kg*	firm	*fr*
consider	*ks*	for (full)	*b*
continue	*ku*	from	*f*
contract	*kc*	full (for)	*b*
contribute	*kb*	general	*jn*
control	*kl*	go (good)	*g*
convenience (convenient)	*kv*	good (go)	*g*
convenient (convenience)	*kv*	grate (great)	*gr*
correspond (correspondence)	*cor*	great (grate)	*gr*
correspondence (correspond)	*cor*	had (he, him)	*h*
customer	*K*	has	*hs*
deliver	*dl*	have (of, very)	*v*
determine	*dl*	he (had, him)	*h*
develop	*dv*	him (had, he)	*h*
difficult	*dfc*	his (is)	*,*
direct (doctor)	*dr*	hospital	*hsp*
distribute	*D*	immediate	*⌢*
doctor (direct)	*dr*	importance (important)	*pl*
during	*du_*	important (importance)	*pl*
employ	*⌐p*	in (not)	*n*
ever (every)	*Є*	include	*l*
every (ever)	*Ɛ*	individual	*Nv*
experience	*γp*	industry	*n*

is (his)	)	own (on)	o
it (at)	/	part (port)	pt
letter	L	participate	pp
manage	~	particular	ptc
manufacture	~	perhaps	Ph
market	~	please (up)	p
more (am)	~	point	py
necessary	nes	port (part)	pt
next	nx	present	p
not (in)	m	property	prp
note	nt	prove	pv
of (have, very)	v	public	pb
on (own)	o	refer	rf
once	oN	respond (response)	rsp
operate	op	response (respond)	rsp
opinion	opn	sample	sa
opportunity	opt	satisfactory (satisfy)	sat
order	od	satisfy (satisfactory)	sat
ordinary	ord	several	sv
organize	og	ship	A
other	ot	signature (significance, significant)	sig
our (are)	r		
over	O		

significance (signature, significant)	*sig*	up (please)	*p*
		us	*s*
significant (signature, significance)	*sig*	usual	*uz*
situate	*sit*	very (have, of)	*v*
specific (specify)	*sp*	was (as)	*z*
specify (specific)	*sp*	we	*e*
standard	*sd*	well (will)	*l*
success	*suc*	were (with)	*‿*
suggest	*sug*	why	*y*
that	*ta*	will (well)	*l*
the	*(*	with (were)	*‿*
they	*ly*	work (world)	*‿o*
those	*loz*	world (work)	*‿od*
to (too)	*l*	would	*d*
too (to)	*l*	your	*u*
under	*u*		

INDEX OF ABBREVIATIONS

ALPHABETICAL LISTING

advertise	*av*	dollars (dollar)	*$*
agriculture	*agr*	east	*E*
America (American)	*a*	economic (economy)	*eco*
American (America)	*a*	economy (economic)	*eco*
amount	*at*	enclose (enclosure)	*enc*
and	*+*	enclosure (enclose)	*enc*
attention	*att*	envelope	*env*
avenue	*ave*	especially	*esp*
billion	*B*	establish	*est*
boulevard	*blvd*	et cetera	*etc*
catalog	*cat*	example (executive)	*ex*
cent (cents)	*¢*	executive (example)	*ex*
cents (cent)	*¢*	federal	*fed*
Christmas	*Xs*	feet	*ft*
company	*co*	government	*gvt*
corporation	*corp*	hour	*hr*
credit	*cr*	hundred	*H*
day	*d*	inch	*in*
department	*dpt*	incorporate (incorporated)	*inc*
dollar (dollars)	*$*	incorporated (incorporate)	*inc*

information	*inf*	question	*q*
insurance	*ins*	record	*rec*
invoice	*inv*	regard	*re*
junior	*jr*	represent (representative)	*rep*
literature	*lit*	representative (represent)	*rep*
merchandise	*dse*	return	*ret*
million	*M*	second (secretary)	*sec*
Miss	*m*	secretary (second)	*sec*
month	*o*	senior	*sr*
Mr.	*r*	south	*S*
Mrs.	*rs*	square	*sq*
Ms.	*s*	street	*S*
north	*N*	superintendent	*S*
number	*no*	thousand	*T*
okay	*ok*	total	*tot*
ounce	*oz*	university	*U*
percent	*%*	vice president	*VP*
pound	*lb*	volume	*vol*
president	*P*	west	*W*
quart	*qt*	yard	*yd*

INDEX OF PHRASES

The following phrases are presented in alphabetical segments beginning with the pronouns I, we, and you plus a verb, followed by infinitive phrases (to plus a verb), high-frequency word combinations, and word combinations with words omitted.

The phrase list presents the 147 phrases in alphabetical segments.

Type	Number
"I" + a verb	25
"We" + a verb	26
"You" + a verb	20
"To" + a verb (infinitive phrase)	24
High-Frequency Word Combinations	44
Words Omitted and Word Compounds with a Word Omitted	8
Total	147

Phrase	Outline	Phrase	Outline
I am	_	I know	*ino*
I appreciate	*iap*	I look	*ilc*
I believe	*iblv*	I shall	*isl*
I can	*ic*	I should	*isd*
I can be	*icb*	I was	*iz*
I cannot	*icn*	I will	*il*
I could	*icd*	I will be	*ilb*
I do	*idu*	I would	*id*
I feel	*ifl*	I would appreciate	*idap*
I had	*ih*	I would be	*idb*
I have	*iv*	I would like	*idlc*
I have been	*ivb*	we appreciate	*eap*
I have had	*ivh*	we are	*er*
I hope	*ihp*	we are not	*ern*

we are pleased	*erp-*	you are	*ur*
we believe	* eblv*	you can	*uc*
we can	*ec*	you cannot	*ucn*
we can be	*ecb*	you can be	*ucb*
we cannot	*ecn*	you could	*ucd*
we could	*ecd*	you do	*udu*
we do	*edu*	you had	*uh*
we feel	*efl*	you have	*uv*
we had	*eh*	you have been	*uvb*
we have	*ev*	you have had	*uvh*
we have been	*evb*	you know	*uno*
we have had	*evh*	you need	*und*
we hope	*ehp*	you should	*usd*
we know	*eno*	you were	*u*
we shall	*esl*	you will	*ul*
we should	*esd*	you will be	*ulb*
we were	*e*	you will find	*ulfn*
we will	*el*	you would	*ud*
we will be	*elb*	you would be	*udb*
we would	*ed*	you would like	*udlc*
we would appreciate	*edap*	to be	*lb*
we would be	*edb*	to call	*lcl*
we would like	*edlc*	to come	*lk*

to determine	*ldl*	as to	*zl*
to do	*ldu*	as we	*ze*
to get	*lgl*	as well as	*zlz*
to give	*lgv*	as you	*zu*
to go	*lq*	as your	*zu*
to have	*lv*	at the	*s*
to have you	*lvu*	can be	*cb*
to have your	*lvu*	could be	*cdb*
to hear	*lhr*	fact that	*fcla*
to keep	*lcp*	for the	*f*
to know	*lno*	for you	*fu*
to make	*lc*	for your	*fu*
to offer	*lofr*	has been	*hsb*
to pay	*lpa*	have been	*vb*
to receive	*lrsv*	have had	*vh*
to say	*lsa*	have not	*vn*
to see	*lse*	have you	*vu*
to send	*lsn*	have your	*vu*
to use	*luz*	in the	*n*
to visit	*lvzl*	it is	*s*
to work	*lo*	of our	*vr*
and the	*r*	of the	*v*
as I	*zl*	of you	*vu*

of your	*vu*	will be	*lb*
on the	*o*	will you	*lu*
on you	*ou*	will your	*lu*
on your	*ou*	would be	*db*
should be	*sdb*	would like	*dlc*
thank you	*lqu*	as soon as	*33*
that I	*lai*	nevertheless	*nvrls*
that we	*lae*	nonetheless	*nnls*
that you	*lau*	thank you for	*lqf*
that you are	*laur*	thank you for your	*lqf*
that you will	*laul*	thank you for your letter	*lqfL*
that your	*lau*	time to time	*Ltt*
to you	*lu*	up to date	*pda*
to your	*lu*		

IDENTIFICATION INITIALS FOR UNITED STATES AND TERRITORIES

Alabama (AL)	AL	Maryland (MD)	MD
Alaska (AK)	AK	Massachusetts (MA)	MA
Arizona (AZ)	AZ	Michigan (MI)	MI
Arkansas (AR)	AR	Minnesota (MN)	MN
California (CA)	CA	Mississippi (MS)	MS
Colorado (CO)	CO	Missouri (MO)	MO
Connecticut (CT)	CT	Montana (MT)	MT
Delaware (DE)	DE	Nebraska (NE)	NE
District of Columbia (DC)	DC	Nevada (NV)	NV
Florida (FL)	FL	New Hampshire (NH)	NH
Georgia (GA)	GA	New Jersey (NJ)	NJ
Hawaii (HI)	HI	New Mexico (NM)	NM
Idaho (ID)	ID	New York (NY)	NY
Illinois (IL)	IL	North Carolina (NC)	NC
Indiana (IN)	IN	North Dakota (ND)	ND
Iowa (IA)	IA	Ohio (OH)	OH
Kansas (KS)	KS	Oklahoma (OK)	OK
Kentucky (KY)	KY	Oregon (OR)	OR
Louisiana (LA)	LA	Pennsylvania (PA)	PA
Maine (ME)	ME	Rhode Island (RI)	RI

South Carolina (SC)	SC	West Virginia (WV)	WV
South Dakota (SD)	SD	Wisconsin (WI)	WI
Tennessee (TN)	TN	Wyoming (WY)	WY
Texas (TX)	TX		
Utah (UT)	UT	Canal Zone (CZ)	CZ
Vermont (VT)	VT	Guam (GU)	GU
Virginia (VA)	VA	Puerto Rico (PR)	PR
Washington (WA)	WA	Virgin Islands (VI)	VI

CANADIAN PROVINCES AND TERRITORIES

Alberta (AB)	*A B*	Nova Scotia (NS)	*NS*
British Columbia (BC)	*BC*	Ontario (ON)	*ON*
Manitoba (MB)	*MB*	Prince Edward Island (PE)	*PE*
New Brunswick (NB)	*NB*	Quebec (PQ)	*PQ*
Newfoundland (NF)	*NF*	Saskatchewan (SK)	*SK*
Northwest Territories (NT)	*NT*	Yukon Territory (YT)	*YT*

METRIC TERMS

	(length) meter *m*	(capacity) liter *l*	(weight) gram *g*
kilo	km	kl	kg
hecto	hm	hl	hg
deca	dam	dal	dag
deci	dm	dl	dg
centi	cm	cl	cg
milli	mm	ml	mg
micro	crm	crl	crg
nano	nm	nl	ng

SUMMARY OF SPEEDWRITING SHORTHAND PRINCIPLES

BY ORDER OF PRESENTATION

1. Write what you hear — high — *hi*

2. Drop medial vowels — build — *bld*

3. Write initial and final vowels — office — *ofs* — fee — *fe*

4. Write C for the sound of k — copy — *cpe*

5. Write a capital C for the sound of ch — check — *Cc*

6. Write $\frown$ for the sound of m — may — *⌢a*

7. Write $\smile$ for the sound of w and wh — way — *⌣a* — when — *⌣n*

8. Underscore the last letter of any outline to add *ing* or *thing* as a word ending — billing — *bl̲* — something — *s̲*

9. To form the plural of any outline ending in a mark of punctuation, double the last mark of punctuation — savings — *sv̳*

10. Write $\jmath$ to form the plural of any outline, to show possession, or to add $\jmath$ to a verb — books — *bcs* — runs — *rns*

11. Write m for the sounds of *mem* and *mum* — memo — *mo*

12. Write m for the sounds of *men, min, mon, mun* — menu — *mu* — money — *me*

13. Write *m* for the word endings *mand, mend, mind, ment*

demand *dm*   amend *am*

remind *rm*   payment *pam*

14. Write a capital *N* for the sound of *nt*

sent *sN*

15. Write *A* for the sound of *ish* or *sh*

finish *fns*

16. Write a capital *a* for the word beginnings *ad, all, al*

admit *ad*   also *aso*

17. Write *m* for the initial sound of *in* or *en*

indent *ndN*

18. Write *o* for the sound of *ow*

allow *alo*

19. Write a printed capital *S* (joined) for the word beginnings *cer, cir, ser, sur*

certain *Sln*   survey *Sva*

20. To form the past tense of a regular verb, write a hyphen after the outline

used *uz-*

21. Write *l* for the sound of *ith* or *th*

them *L*

22. Write *l* for the word ending *ly* or *ily*

family *ful*

23. Write a capital *D* for the word beginning *dis*

discuss *Dcs*

24. Write a capital *M* for the word beginning *mis*

misplace *Mpls*

25. Retain beginning or ending vowels when building compound words

payroll *parl*   headache *hdac*

26. Retain root-word vowels when adding prefixes and suffixes

disappear *Dapr*   payment *pam*

159

27. Write a capital *P* (disjoined) for the word beginnings *per, pur, pre, pro, pro* (prah)

person *Psn* prepare *Ppr*

provide *Pvd* problem *Pbl*

28. Write *q* for the word ending *gram*

telegram *Ulq*

29. Write *y* for the sound of *oi*

boy *by*

30. For words ending in a long vowel + *t*, omit the *t* and write the vowel

rate *ra* meet *⌒e*

31. Write *a* for the word beginning *an*

answer *asr*

32. Write *q* for the medial or final sound of any vowel + *nk*

bank *bq* link *lq*

33. Write a capital *S* (disjoined) for the word beginning *super* and for the word endings *scribe* and *script*

supervise *Svz* describe *dS*

manuscript *⌒mS*

34. Write *el* for the word beginning *electr*

electronic *elnc*

35. Write *w* for the word ending *ward*

backward *bcw*

36. Write *h* for the word ending *hood*

boyhood *byh*

37. Write */* for the word ending *tion* or *sion*

vacation *vcy*

38. Write *a* for the initial and final sound of *aw*

law *la* audit *adl*

39. Write *q* for the sound of *kw*

quick *qc*

40. Write a capital *N* for the sound of *nd*

friend *frN*

41. Write *⌒* for the initial sound of *em* or *im*

emphasize *fsz* impress *prs*

42. Omit *p* in the sound of *mpt*   prompt   *P⌐ι*

43. Write   *k*   for the sounds of *com,*   common   *kn*   convey   *kva*
    con, coun, count   counsel   *ksl*   account   *ak*

44. Write   *S*   for the sound of *st*   rest   *rS*

45. Write   *q*   for the word ending
    quire   require   *rq*

46. Write   *3*   for the sound of *zh*   pleasure   *pl3r*

47. Write   *´*   for the word ending
    ness   kindness   *cN´*

48. Write   \   for words beginning
    with the sound of any vowel + *x*   explain   *↘pln*   accident   *vdN*

49. Write   *⋌*   for the medial and final
    sound of *x*   boxes   *bⅹs*   relax   *rlⅹ*

50. Write   *X*   for the word beginnings   extreme   *X⌐*
    extr and *extra*   extraordinary   *Xord*

51. Write   *q*   for the medial or final
    sound of any vowel + *ng*   rang   *rq*   single   *sgl*

52. Write   *B*   for the word endings
    bil, ble, bly   possible   *psB*   probably   *PbB*

53. Omit the final *t* of a root word after
    the sound of *k*   act   *ac*

54. Write a slightly raised and disjoined
       ι   for the word ending *ity*   quality   *ql´ι*

55. Write   *U*   for the word beginning
    un   until   *ull*

56. Write   *sl*   for the sound of *shul*
    and for the word ending *chul*   financial   *fnnsl*

57. Write *M* for the sounds of *ance,*
    ence, nce, nse   expense

58. Write *S* for the word beginning
    sub   submit

59. Write *V* for the medial and final
    sound of *tive*   effective

60. Write *ʃ* for the word endings
    ful and *ify*   careful   justify

61. Write *ʃ* for the word ending
    ification   qualifications

62. Write a capital *N* for the word   enterprise
    beginnings *enter, inter, intro*
                                              introduce   interest

63. Write *ʃ* for the word beginning
    and ending *self*   self-made   myself

64. Write *sv* for the word ending
    selves   ourselves

65. When a word contains two medial,
    consecutively pronounced vowels,
    write the first vowel   trial

66. When a word ends in two
    consecutively pronounced vowels,
    write only the last vowel   idea

67. Write *T* for the word beginnings
    tran and *trans*   transfer